iPhone™

FOR

DUMMIES®

2ND EDITION

iPhone™

FOR

DUMMIES®

2ND EDITION

by Edward C. Baig

USA TODAY Personal Tech columnist,

and Bob LeVitus

Houston Chronicle "Dr. Mac" columnist

Wiley Publishing, Inc.

iPhone™ For Dummies®, 2nd Edition

Published by
Wiley Publishing, Inc.
111 River Street
Hoboken, NJ 07030-5774
www.wiley.com

WILEY

About the Authors

Edward C. Baig writes the weekly Personal Technology column in *USA TODAY* and is co-host of the weekly *USA TODAY*'s Talking Tech podcast with Jefferson Graham. Ed is also the author of *Macs For Dummies,* 10th Ed. (Wiley Publishing). Before joining *USA TODAY* as a columnist and reporter in 1999, Ed spent six years at *Business Week,* where he wrote and edited stories about consumer tech, personal finance, collectibles, travel, and wine tasting, among other topics. He received the Medill School of Journalism 1999 Financial Writers and Editors Award for contributions to the "*Business Week* Investor Guide to Online Investing." That followed a three-year stint at *U.S. News & World Report,* where Ed was the lead tech writer for the News You Can Use section but also dabbled in numerous other subjects.

Ed began his journalist career at *Fortune* magazine, gaining the best basic training imaginable during his early years as a fact checker and contributor to the Fortune 500. Through the dozen years he worked at the magazine, Ed covered leisure-time industries, penned features on the lucrative "dating" market and the effect of religion on corporate managers, and was heavily involved in the Most Admired Companies project. Ed also started up Fortune's Products to Watch column, a venue for low- and high-tech items.

Bob LeVitus, often referred to as "Dr. Mac," has written or co-written more than 50 popular computer books, including *Mac OS X Leopard For Dummies* and *Microsoft Office 2008 for Mac For Dummies* for Wiley Publishing, Inc.; *Stupid Mac Tricks* and *Dr. Macintosh* for Addison-Wesley; and *The Little iTunes Book*, 3rd Edition, and *The Little iDVD Book*, 2nd Edition, for Peachpit Press. His books have sold more than one million copies worldwide. Bob has penned the popular Dr. Mac column for the *Houston Chronicle* for the past ten years and has been published in pretty much every magazine that ever used the word *Mac* in its title. His achievements have been documented in major media around the world. (Yes, that was him juggling a keyboard in *USA TODAY* a few years back!)

Bob is known for his expertise, trademark humorous style, and ability to translate techie jargon into usable and fun advice for regular folks. Bob is also a prolific public speaker, presenting more than 100 Macworld Expo training sessions in the U.S. and abroad, keynote addresses in three countries, and Macintosh training seminars in many U.S. cities.

Dedications

I dedicate this book to my beautiful wife, Janie, for making me a better person every day I am with her. And to my incredible kids: my adorable little girl, Sydney (one of her first words was "iPod,") my little boy, Sammy (who is all smiles from the moment he wakes up in the morning), and, of course, my "canine" son, Eddie. They all got their hands on the iPhone at one time or another. I am madly in love with you all.

— Ed Baig

This book is dedicated to my wife, Lisa, who taught me almost everything I know about almost everything except computers. And to my children, Allison and Jacob, who love their iPhones almost as much as I love them (my kids, not my iPhone).

— Bob LeVitus

Authors' Acknowledgments

Special thanks to everyone at Apple who helped us turn this book around so quickly: Katie Cotton, Natalie Kerris, Greg (Joz) Joswiak, Bob Borchers, John Richey, Keri Walker, Teresa Brewer, Jennifer Hakes, Jennifer Bowcock, and everyone else. We couldn't have done it without you.

Big-time thanks to the gang at Wiley: Bob "Can't you work any faster?" Woerner, Jodi "Is that _____ done yet?" Jensen, Andy "The Boss" Cummings, Barry "Still no humorous nickname" Pruett, and our technical editor Dennis R. Cohen, who did a rocking job in record time as always. Finally, thanks to everyone at Wiley we don't know by name. If you helped with this project in any way, you have our everlasting thanks.

Bob adds: Thanks also to super-agent Carole "Still Swifty in my book" McClendon, for deal-making beyond the call of duty, yet again. You've been my agent for over 20 years and you're *still* the best. And thanks also to my family and friends for putting up with me throughout my hibernation during this book's gestation. Finally, thanks to Brooklyn Pie Company and Home Slice for killer thin-crust pizza, The Iron Works for BBQ beef ribs beyond compare, Chuy's for burritos as big as yo' face, ShortStop for cheap, tasty burgers, and Diet Vanilla Coke Zero because it's awesome.

Ed adds: Thanks to my agent Matt Wagner for again turning me into a *Dummies* author. It is a privilege to be working with you again. I'd also like to thank Jim Henderson, Geri Tucker, Nancy Blair and the rest of my *USA TODAY* friends and colleagues (in and out of the Money section) for your enormous support and encouragement. Most of all, thanks to my loving family for understanding my nightly (and weekend) disappearances as we raced to get this project completed on time.

And finally, thanks to you, gentle reader, for buying our book.

Publisher's Acknowledgments

We're proud of this book; please send us your comments through our online registration form located at www.dummies.com/register/.

Some of the people who helped bring this book to market include the following:

Acquisitions and Editorial

Project Editor: Jodi Jensen

Executive Editor: Bob Woerner

Copy Editor: Barry Childs-Helton

Technical Editor: Dennis Cohen

Editorial Manager: Jodi Jensen

Editorial Assistant: Amanda Foxworth

Sr. Editorial Assistant: Cherie Case

Cartoons: Rich Tennant (www.the5thwave.com)

Composition Services

Project Coordinator: Kristie Rees

Layout and Graphics: Ana Carrillo, Carrie A. Cesavice, Christine Williams

Proofreaders: Debbye Butler, Dwight Ramsey, Amanda Steiner

Indexer: Broccoli Information Management

Special Help

Annie Sullivan

Publishing and Editorial for Technology Dummies

Richard Swadley, Vice President and Executive Group Publisher

Andy Cummings, Vice President and Publisher

Mary Bednarek, Executive Acquisitions Director

Mary C. Corder, Editorial Director

Publishing for Consumer Dummies

Diane Graves Steele, Vice President and Publisher

Composition Services

Gerry Fahey, Vice President of Production Services

Debbie Stailey, Director of Composition Services

Contents at a Glance

Table of Contents

Introduction

*P*recious few products ever come close to generating the kind of buzz seen with the iPhone. Its messianic arrival received front-page treatment in newspapers and top billing on network and cable TV shows. People lined up days in advance just to ensure landing one of the first units. Years from now, people will insist, "I was one of them."

But we trust you didn't pick up this book to read yet another account about how the iPhone launch was an epochal event. We trust you *did* buy the book to find out how to get the very most out of your remarkable new device.

Our goal is to deliver that information in a light and breezy fashion. We expect you to have fun using your iPhone. We equally hope you have fun spending time with us.

About This Book

Let's get one thing out of the way right from the get-go. We think you're pretty darn smart for buying a *For Dummies* book. That says to us that you have the confidence and intelligence to know what you don't know. The *For Dummies* franchise is built around the core notion that all of us feel insecure about certain topics when tackling them for the first time, especially when those topics have to do with technology.

As with most products coming out of Apple, the iPhone is beautifully designed and intuitive to use. And though our editors may not want us to reveal this dirty little secret (especially on the first page, for goodness sake), the truth is you'll get pretty far just by exploring the iPhone's many functions and features on your own, without the help of this or any other book.

Okay, now that we spilled the beans, let's tell you why you shouldn't run back to the bookstore and request a refund. This book is chock-full of useful tips, advice, and other nuggets that should make your iPhone experience all the more pleasurable. So keep this book nearby and consult it often.

Conventions Used in This Book

First, we want to tell you how we go about our business. *iPhone For Dummies,* 2nd Edition, makes generous use of numbered steps, bullet lists, and pictures. Web addresses are shown in a special monofont typeface, `like this`.

We also include a few sidebars with information that is not required reading (not that any of this book is) but that we hope will provide a richer understanding of certain subjects. Overall, we aim to keep technical jargon to a minimum, under the guiding principle that with rare exceptions you don't need to know what any of it really means.

How This Book Is Organized

Here's something we imagine you've never heard before: Most books have a beginning, middle, and end, and you do well to adhere to that linear structure — unless you're one of those knuckleheads out to ruin it for the rest of us by revealing that the butler did it.

Fortunately, there is no ending to spoil in a *For Dummies* book. So although you may want to digest this book from start to finish — and we hope you do — we won't penalize you for skipping ahead or jumping around. Having said that, we organized *iPhone For Dummies,* 2nd Ed., in an order that we think makes the most sense, as follows.

Part 1: Getting to Know Your iPhone

In the introductory chapters of Part I, you tour the iPhone inside and out, find out how to activate the phone with Apple's partner in the U.S., AT&T, and get hands-on (or, more precisely, fingers-on) experience with the iPhone's unique virtual multitouch display.

Part II: The Mobile iPhone

There's a reason the iPhone has phone in its name. Part II is mostly about all the ways you can make and receive calls on the device. But you also discover how to exchange text messages and play with the Calendar, Clock, and Calculator applications.

Part III: The Multimedia iPhone

Part III is where the fun truly begins. This is the iPhone as an iPod, meaning that music, videos, movies, pictures, and other diversions come to life.

Part IV: The Internet iPhone

Part IV covers the mobile Internet. You master the Safari browser, e-mail, maps, and more. We discuss the faster 3G or third-generation wireless network that the latest iPhone can tap into. And, speaking of maps, your iPhone has the capability to locate your whereabouts through GPS (in the case of the iPhone 3G) and other location-tracking methods.

Part V: The Undiscovered iPhone

In Part V, you find out how to apply your preferences through the iPhone's internal settings, how to find and obtain new applications at the iTunes App Store, and discover where to go for troubleshooting assistance if your iPhone should misbehave.

Part VI: The Part of Tens

The Part of Tens: Otherwise known as the *For Dummies* answer to David Letterman. The lists presented in Part VI steer you to some of our favorite iPhone apps, a bevy of terrific iPhone-related Web sites, and last, but not least, some handy tips and shortcuts.

Icons Used in This Book

Little round pictures (icons) appear in the left margins throughout this book. Consider these icons miniature road signs, telling you a little something extra about the topic at hand or really hammering a point home.

Here's what the four different icons used in this book look like and mean.

These are the juicy morsels, shortcuts, and recommendations that might make the task at hand faster or easier.

This tip emphasizes the stuff we think you ought to retain. You may even jot down a note to yourself in the iPhone.

Put on your propeller beanie hat and pocket protector; this text includes the truly geeky stuff. You can safely ignore this material; but if it weren't interesting or informative, we wouldn't have bothered to write it.

You wouldn't intentionally run a stop sign, would you? In the same fashion, ignoring warnings may be hazardous to your iPhone and (by extension) your wallet. There, you now know how these warning icons work, for you have just received your very first warning!

Where to Go from Here

Why straight to Chapter 1, of course, (without passing Go).

In all seriousness, we wrote this book for you, so please let us know what you think. If we screwed up, confused you, left something out, or — heaven forbid — made you angry, drop us a note. And if we hit you with one pun too many, it helps to know that as well.

Because writers are people too (believe it or not), we also encourage positive feedback if you think it's warranted. So kindly send e-mail to Ed at baigdummies@aol.com and to Bob at iPhoneLeVitus@boblevitus.com. We'll do our best to respond to reasonably polite e-mail in a timely fashion.

Most of all, we want to thank you for buying our book. Please enjoy it along with your new iPhone.

Note: At the time we wrote this book, all the information it contained was accurate for the original iPhone, the iPhone 3G, and the latest version of iTunes. Apple is likely to introduce a new iPhone model or new version of iTunes between book editions. If you've bought a new iPhone or your version of iTunes looks a little different, be sure to check out what Apple has to say at www.apple.com/iPhone. You'll no doubt find updates on the company's latest releases.

Part I
Getting to Know Your iPhone

The 5th Wave — By Rich Tennant

"Other than this little glitch with the landscape view, I really love my iPhone."

*Y*ou have to crawl before you walk, so consider this part basic training for crawling. The three chapters that make up Part I serve as a gentle introduction to your iPhone.

We start out nice and easy in Chapter 1, with a big-picture overview, even letting you know what's in the box (if you haven't already peeked). Then we examine just some of the cool things your iPhone can do. We finish things off with a quick-and-dirty tour of the hardware and the software, so that you'll know where things are when you need them.

Next, after you're somewhat familiar with where things are and what they do, we move right along to a bunch of useful iPhone skills, such as turning the darn thing on and off (which is very important) and locking and unlocking your phone (which is also very important). Chapter 2 ends with useful tips and tricks to help you master iPhone's unique multitouch interface so that you can use it effectively and efficiently.

Then, in Chapter 3, we explore the process of synchronization and how to get data — contacts, appointments, movies, songs, podcasts, and such — from your computer into your iPhone, quickly and painlessly.

Photo credits:
©iStockphoto.com/iLexx (Top)
©iStockphoto.com/Tina Rencelj (Middle)
©iStockphoto.com/Serega (Bottom)

Unveiling the iPhone

*C*ongratulations. You've selected one of the most incredible handheld devices we've ever seen — and one that's much more than just a great wireless phone. Of course, the iPhone is one heck of a wireless telephone, complete with a capable 2-megapixel digital camera. But it's actually *three* awesome handheld devices in one. In addition to being a killer cell phone, it's a gorgeous widescreen video iPod — and the smallest, most powerful Internet communications device yet.

In this chapter, we offer a gentle introduction to all three "products" that make up your iPhone, plus overviews of its revolutionary hardware and software features.

The Big Picture

The iPhone has many best-of-class features, but perhaps its most unusual feature is the lack of a physical keyboard or stylus. Instead, it has a 3¹/₂-inch super-high-resolution touchscreen (160 pixels per inch if you care about such things) that you operate using a pointing device you're already intimately familiar with: your finger.

And what a display it is. We venture that you've never seen a more beautiful screen on a handheld device in your life.

Another feature that knocked our socks off was the iPhone's built-in sensors. An accelerometer detects when you rotate the device from portrait to

What's in the box

Somehow we think you've already opened the handsome black box that the iPhone came in. But if you didn't, here's what you can expect to find inside:

- **Stereo headset:** Use this headset for music videos and, yes, phone calls. The headset contains a built-in microphone for making yourself heard during phone calls.

- **Dock connector–to–USB cable:** Use this handy cable to sync or charge your iPhone. You can plug the USB connector into your PC or Macintosh to sync or plug it into the USB power adapter described next.

- **USB power adapter:** Use this adapter to recharge your iPhone from a standard AC power outlet.

- **Some Apple logo decals:** Of course.

- **Cleaning cloth:** Expect the iPhone to get smudges on it. Use the cloth to wipe it clean. We'd steer clear of Lemon Pledge.

- ***Finger Tips* pamphlet:** You'll find handy tips from Apple on using the new object of your affection.

- ***Important Product Information Guide* pamphlet:** Well, it must be important because it says so right on the cover. You'll find basic safety warnings, a bunch of legalese, warranty information, and info on how to dispose of or recycle the iPhone. *What! We're getting rid of it already?* A few other pieces of advice: Don't drop the iPhone if you can help it, keep the thing dry, and — as with all cell phones — give full attention to the road while driving.

- **SIM eject tool:** Use this tool instead of a bent paper clip in the event you need to eject your SIM card.

  There's even a handy diagram showing how to use the SIM eject tool inside the little black folder the tool is affixed to.

- **iPhone:** You were starting to worry. Yes, the iPhone itself is also in the box.

landscape mode and adjusts what's on the display accordingly. A proximity sensor detects when the iPhone gets near your face, so it can turn off the display to save power and prevent accidental touches by your cheek. And a light sensor adjusts the display's brightness in response to the current ambient lighting situation. (Let's see your Palm Treo or RIM Blackberry do *that!*)

In this section, we take a brief look at some of the iPhone's features, broken down by product category.

The iPhone as a phone and a digital camera

On the phone side, the iPhone synchronizes with the contacts and calendars on your Mac or PC. It includes a full-featured QWERTY soft, or virtual, keyboard, which makes typing text easier than ever before — for some folks. Granted, the virtual keyboard takes a bit of time to get used to. But we think that many of you eventually will be whizzing along at a much faster pace than you thought possible on a mobile keyboard of this type.

The 2-megapixel digital camera is accompanied by a decent photo-management application, so taking and managing digital photos is a pleasure rather than the nightmare it can be on other phones. Plus, you can automatically synchronize iPhone photos with the digital photo library on your Mac or PC. Okay, we wish the iPhone camera took better photos and could capture video, but it's still way better than no camera at all.

Finally, one of our favorite phone accoutrements is visual voicemail. (Try saying that three times fast.) This feature lets you see a list of voicemail messages and choose which ones to listen to or delete without being forced to deal with every message in your voice mailbox in sequential order. Now, *that's* handy!

Those are merely a few of the iPhone's excellent telephony features. Because we still have many more chapters to go, we'll put the phone coverage on hold for now (pun intended).

The iPhone as an iPod

We agree with Steve Jobs on this one: The iPhone is a better iPod than almost any that Apple has ever made. (Okay, we can quibble about the iPod Touch or wanting more storage.) You can enjoy all of your existing iPod content — music, audiobooks, audio and video podcasts, music videos, television shows, and movies — on the iPhone's gorgeous high-resolution color display, which is bigger, brighter, and richer than any iPod display that came before it.

Bottom line: If you can get the content — be it video, audio, or whatever — into iTunes on your Mac or PC, you can synchronize it and watch or listen to it on your iPhone.

The iPhone as an Internet communications device

But wait — there's more! Not only is the iPhone a great phone and a stellar iPod, but it's also a full-featured Internet communications device with — we're about to drop a bit of industry jargon on you — a rich HTML e-mail client that's compatible with most POP and IMAP mail services, with support for Microsoft Exchange ActiveSync. (For more on this topic, see Chapter 11.) Also on board is a world-class Web browser (Safari) that, unlike other phones, makes Web surfing fun and easy.

Another cool Internet feature is Maps, a killer mapping application based on Google Maps. By using GPS (3G hardware) or triangulation (on the original iPhone), it can determine your location, let you view maps and satellite imagery, and obtain driving directions and traffic information regardless of where in the United States you happen to be. You can also find businesses such as gas stations, pizza restaurants, hospitals, and Apple stores with just a few taps.

You might also enjoy using Stocks, a built-in application that delivers near-real-time stock quotes and charts any time and any place.

In other words, the Internet experience on an iPhone is far superior to the Internet experience on any other handheld device.

Technical specifications

One last thing before we proceed. Here's a list of everything you need before you can actually *use* your iPhone:

- An original iPhone or the newer iPhone 3G
- A wireless contract with AT&T (formerly Cingular)
- Internet access (required) — broadband wireless Internet access recommended

Plus you need one of the following:

- A Mac with a USB 2.0 port; Mac OS X version 10.4.10 or later; and iTunes 7.7 or later
- A PC with a USB 2.0 port; Windows Vista or Windows XP Home or Professional with Service Pack 2 or later; and iTunes 7.7 or later

A Quick Tour Outside

The iPhone is a harmonious combination of hardware and software, so let's see just what it's made of. In this section, we take a brief look at what's on the outside. In the next section, we peek at the software.

On the top

On the top of your iPhone, you'll find the headset jack, the SIM card tray, and the Sleep/Wake button, as shown in Figure 1-1:

- **The Sleep/Wake button:** This button is used to lock or unlock your iPhone and to turn your iPhone on or off. When your iPhone is locked, you can still receive calls and text messages but nothing happens if you touch its screen. When your iPhone is turned off, all incoming calls go directly to voicemail.

✔ **SIM card tray:** The SIM card tray is where you remove or replace the SIM card inside your iPhone.

A SIM (Subscriber Identity Module) card is a removable smart card used to identify mobile phones. It allows users to change phones by moving the SIM card from one phone to another.

✔ **Headset jack:** The headset jack lets you plug in the included iPhone headset, which looks a lot like white iPod earbuds. Unlike the iPod ear-buds, however, the iPhone headset has a microphone so that you can talk as well as listen.

The headset jack on the *original* iPhone is recessed, so most third-party earphones (such as those made by Shure, Etymotic, and Future Sonics) won't work with it. Starting at around $11, however, you can buy an adapter from companies such as Belkin that enables you to use just about any brand or style of earphones you like with your iPhone. Fortunately, Apple listened to customers. The iPhone 3G doesn't have a recessed headset jack and doesn't require an adapter.

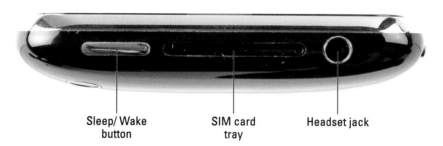

Sleep/Wake button   SIM card tray   Headset jack

Figure 1-1: The top side of the iPhone 3G.

On the bottom

On the bottom of your iPhone, you'll find the speaker, dock connector, and microphone, as shown in Figure 1-2:

✔ **Speaker:** The speaker is used by the iPhone's built-in speakerphone and plays audio — music or video soundtracks — if no headset is plugged in. It also plays the ringtone you hear when you receive a call.

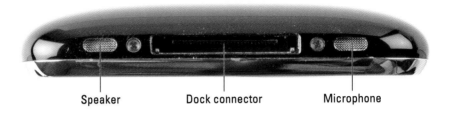

Speaker   Dock connector   Microphone

Figure 1-2: The bottom side of the iPhone 3G.

🔌 **Dock connector:** The dock connector has two purposes. One, you can use it to recharge your iPhone's battery: Simply connect one end of the included dock connector–to–USB cable to the dock connector and the other end to the USB power adapter. Two, you can use the dock connector to recharge your iPhone's battery as well as synchronize: Connect one end of the same cable to the dock connector and the other end to a USB port on your Mac or PC.

🔌 **Microphone:** The microphone lets callers hear your voice when you're not using a headset.

On the sides and front

On the front of your iPhone you'll find the following (labeled in Figure 1-3):

🔌 **Ring/Silent switch:** The Ring/Silent switch, which is on the left side of your iPhone, lets you quickly switch between ring mode and silent mode. When the switch is set to ring mode — the up position, with no orange dot — your iPhone plays all sounds through the speaker on the bottom. When the switch is set to silent mode — the down position, with an orange dot visible on the switch — your iPhone doesn't make a sound when you receive a call or when an alert pops up on the screen.

The only exceptions to silent mode are alarms you set in the built-in Clock application, which do sound regardless of the Ring/Silent switch setting.

If your phone is set to ring mode and you want to silence it quickly, you can press the Sleep/Wake button on the top of the iPhone or press one of the Volume buttons.

🔌 **Volume buttons:** Two Volume buttons are just below the Ring/Silent switch. The upper button increases the volume, the lower one decreases it. You use the Volume buttons to raise or lower the loudness of the ringer, alerts, sound effects, songs, and movies. And during phone calls, they adjust the loudness of the person you're speaking with, regardless of whether you're listening through the receiver, the speakerphone, or a headset.

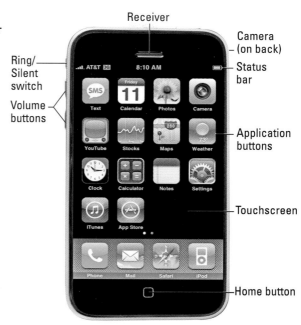

▶ **Receiver:** The receiver is the speaker that the iPhone uses for telephone calls. It naturally sits close to your ear whenever you hold your iPhone in the "talking on the phone" position.

You should be the only one who hears sound coming from the receiver. If you have the volume set above about 50 percent and you're in a location with little or no background noise, someone standing nearby may be able to hear the sound, too. So be careful.

If you require privacy during phone calls, the included Apple headset (or an optional Bluetooth headset — as discussed in Chapter 13) is a better bet.

Figure 1-3: The front of the iPhone 3G is a study in elegant simplicity.

▶ **Touchscreen:** You find out how to use the iPhone's gorgeous high-resolution color touchscreen in Chapter 2. All we have to say at this time is . . . try not to drool all over it.

▶ **Home button:** No matter what you're doing, you can press the Home button at any time to display the Home screen, which is the screen shown in Figure 1-3.

▶ **Application buttons:** Each of the 18 buttons launches an included iPhone application. You'll read more about these applications later in this chapter and throughout the rest of the book.

On the back

On the back of your iPhone is the camera lens. It's the little circle in the top-left corner. For more on the camera, see Chapter 9.

Status bar

The status bar, which is at the top of the screen, displays tiny icons that provide a variety of information about the current state of your iPhone:

 - **Cell signal:** The cell-signal icon tells you whether you're within range of your wireless telephone carrier's cellular network and therefore can make and receive calls. The more bars you see (five is the highest), the stronger the cellular signal. If you're out of range, the bars are replaced with the words *No service.*

    If you have only one or two bars, try moving around a little bit. Even moving just a few feet can sometimes mean the difference between no service and three or four bars.

 - **Airplane Mode:** You're allowed to use your iPod on a plane after the captain gives the word. But you can't use your cell phone except when the plane is in the gate area before takeoff or after landing. Fortunately, your iPhone offers an Airplane Mode, which turns off all wireless features of your iPhone — the cellular, 3G, GPRS, and EDGE networks, Wi-Fi, and Bluetooth — and makes it possible to enjoy music or video during your flight.

 - **3G:** This icon informs you that the high-speed 3G data network from your wireless carrier (that's AT&T in the U.S.) is available and that your iPhone can connect to the Internet via 3G.

 - **GPRS:** This icon says that your wireless carrier's GPRS (General Packet Radio Service) data network is available and that your iPhone can use it to connect to the Internet.

 - **EDGE:** This icon tells you that your wireless carrier's EDGE network is available and you can use it to connect to the Internet.

 - **Wi-Fi:** If you see the Wi-Fi icon, it means your iPhone is connected to the Internet over a Wi-Fi network. The more semicircular lines you see (up to three), the stronger the Wi-Fi signal. If you have only one or two semicircles of Wi-Fi strength, try moving around a bit. If you don't see the Wi-Fi icon in the status bar, Internet access is not currently available.

Wireless (that is, cellular) carriers may offer one of three data networks. The fastest is a 3G data network, which, as you probably guessed, is available only on the iPhone 3G. The device first looks for a 3G network and then, if it can't find one, looks for a slower EDGE or GPRS data network.

Wi-Fi networks, however, are even faster than any cellular data network — 3G, EDGE, or GPRS. So all iPhones will connect to a Wi-Fi network if one is available, even if a 3G, GPRS, or EDGE network is also available.

Last but not least, if you *don't* see one of these icons — 3G, GPRS, EDGE, or Wi-Fi — then you don't currently have Internet access.

⚬ **Network Activity:** This icon tells you that some network activity is occurring, such as over-the-air synchronization, sending or receiving e-mail, or loading a Web page. Some third-party applications also use this icon to indicate network or other activity.

 ⚬ **VPN:** This icon shows that you are currently connected to a virtual private network (*VPN*).

 ⚬ **Lock:** This icon tells you when your iPhone is locked. See Chapter 2 for information on locking and unlocking your iPhone.

 ⚬ **Play:** This icon informs you that a song is currently playing. You find out more about playing songs in Chapter 7.

 ⚬ **Alarm:** This icon tells you that you have set one or more alarms in the Clock application.

 ⚬ **Bluetooth:** This icon indicates the current state of your iPhone's Bluetooth connection. If it's blue, Bluetooth is on and a device (such as a wireless headset or car kit) is connected. If the icon is gray, Bluetooth is turned on but no device is connected. If you don't see a Bluetooth icon at all, Bluetooth is turned off. Chapter 13 goes into more detail about Bluetooth.

 ⚬ **Bluetooth Headset battery:** This icon displays the battery level for your optional *Apple iPhone Bluetooth headset* (S.R.P. $99) if you have one and it's currently paired with your iPhone.

 ⚬ **Battery:** This icon reflects the level of your battery's charge. It's completely filled with green when your battery is fully charged, and then empties out as your battery becomes depleted. You'll see a lightning bolt inside it when your iPhone is recharging.

 ⚬ **TTY:** This icon informs you that your iPhone is set up to work with a teletype (TTY) machine for those who are hearing- or speech-impaired.

You need an optional *Apple iPhone TTY Adapter* (SRP $19) to connect your iPhone to a TTY machine.

The iPhone's Elegant Eighteen

Tap the Home button at any time to summon your iPhone's Home screen. The Home screen offers 18 icons by default, each representing a different built-in application or function. Because the rest of the book covers each and every one of these babies in full and loving detail, we merely provide brief descriptions here.

Three steps let you rearrange icons on your iPhone:

1. **Press and hold any icon until all of the icons begin to "wiggle."**

2. **Drag the icons around until you're happy with their positions.**

3. **Press the Home button to save your arrangement and stop "wiggling."**

If you haven't rearranged your icons, you'll see the following applications on your Home screen, starting at the top left:

- **Text:** The Text application lets you exchange text messages with almost any other cell phone user. We've used a lot of mobile phones in our day and this application is as good as it gets.

- **Calendar:** No matter what calendar program you prefer on your PC or Mac (as long as it's iCal, Microsoft Entourage, or Microsoft Outlook), you can synchronize events and alerts between your computer and your iPhone. Create an event on one and it's automatically synchronized with the other the next time they're connected. Neat stuff.

- **Photos:** This application is the iPhone's terrific photo manager. You can view pictures that you take with the iPhone's built-in camera or photos transferred from your computer. You can zoom in or out, create slide-shows, e-mail photos to friends, and much more. Other phones may let you take pictures; the iPhone lets you enjoy them in many ways.

- **Camera:** Use this application when you want to shoot a picture with the iPhone's 2-megapixel camera.

- **YouTube:** This application lets you watch videos from the popular YouTube Web site. You can search for a particular video or browse through thousands of offerings. It's a great way to waste a lot of time.

- **Stocks:** If you follow the market, this application lets you monitor your favorite stocks, which are updated in near-real time.

- **Maps:** This application is among our favorites. View street maps or satellite imagery of locations around the globe, or ask for directions, traffic conditions, or even the location of a nearby pizza joint.

- **Weather:** This application monitors the six-day weather forecast for as many cities as you like.

- **Clock:** This program lets you see the current time in as many cities as you like, set one or more alarms for yourself, and use your iPhone as a stopwatch or a countdown timer.

- **Calculator:** The Calculator application lets you perform addition, subtraction, multiplication, and division. Period.

- **Notes:** This program lets you type notes while you're out and about. You can send the notes to yourself or anyone else through e-mail or just save them on your iPhone until you need them.

- **Settings:** Use this application to adjust your iPhone's settings. If you're a Mac user, think System Preferences; if you're a Windows person, think Control Panel.

- ✓ **iTunes:** Tap here to access the iTunes Wi-Fi Music Store where you can browse, preview, and purchase songs, albums, and more.

- ✓ **App Store:** This icon enables you to connect to and search the iTunes App Store for iPhone applications you can purchase or download for free over Wi-Fi or cellular data network connection.

- ✓ **Phone:** Tap this application icon to use the iPhone as a phone. What a concept!

- ✓ **Mail:** This application lets you send and receive e-mail with most POP3 and IMAP e-mail systems.

- ✓ **Safari:** Safari is your Web browser. If you're a Mac user, you know that already; if you're a Windows user, think Internet Explorer on steroids.

- ✓ **iPod:** Last but not least, this icon unleashes all the power of a video iPod right on your phone.

Okay, then. Now that you and your iPhone have been properly introduced, it's time to turn it on, activate it, and actually use it. Onward!

iPhone Basic Training

In This Chapter

▷ Activating the iPhone

▷ Turning the device on and off

▷ Locking your iPhone

▷ Mastering multitouch

*B*y now you know that the iPhone is very different from other cell phones. If you got caught up in the initial iPhone frenzy of 2007, you may have plotted for months about how to land one. After all, the iPhone quickly emerged as the ultimate fashion phone. And the chic device hosted a bevy of cool features. (Keep reading this book for proof.)

To snag the very first version, you may have saved up your pennies or said, "The budget be damned." Owning the hippest and most-hyped handset on the planet came at a premium cost compared with rival devices.

Something else was different about the iPhone purchasing experience in 2007: the way it was activated. No salesperson was going to guide you through the process, whether you picked up your newly prized possession in an Apple retail store, an AT&T retail store, or on the Web. Instead, you had to handle activation solo, in the comfort of your own home.

Unless you were among those people who experienced activation hiccups in the days soon after the phone was released in June 2007, the process of getting up to speed with the iPhone was (for the most part) dirt simple and fun — as it is with most products with an Apple pedigree.

Well, forget all that has gone before. You no longer have to break the bank. Apple has lowered the price — a lot.

©iStockphoto.com/DRabPics

As of this writing, the cheapest iPhone starts at $199 — $400 below its stratospheric launch price. (Though we are obliged to point out that AT&T's monthly service plans are higher — thus eliminating the cost savings over the course of the required two-year contract.)

Something else has changed — the way you activate the phone. Kindly read on.

Activating the iPhone

You're now supposed to activate the iPhone in the Apple or AT&T Wireless store where you bought the thing, just as you do with other cell phones. You'll choose your desired monthly bucket of voice minutes and SMS or text messages.

If you're already an AT&T subscriber, the salesperson will give you the option of keeping your current phone number.

It's not surprising why Apple and AT&T want you in their stores: After they get you in the door, they have the opportunity to sell you other stuff. And they can help crack down on those techies who want to unlock or "jailbreak" the iPhone to defect to a rival carrier.

Otherwise, this time around, the same two prerequisites for enjoying the iPhone are in place as with the original release — at least for U.S. customers. First, there's the aforementioned business of becoming an AT&T (formerly Cingular) subscriber, unless you're already in the fold. You'll have to ink that new two-year term. If you're in the middle of a contract with a rival carrier, read the sidebar titled "The Great Escape: Bailing out of your wireless contract."

Second, make sure you download the latest version of iTunes software onto your PC or Mac. Apple doesn't supply the software in the box, so head to www.apple.com/itunes if you need to fetch a copy, or launch your current version of iTunes and then choose Check for Updates. You can find it under the Help menu on a Windows machine and on the iTunes menu on a Mac.

For the uninitiated, iTunes is the nifty Apple jukebox software that iPod owners and many other people use to manage music, videos, and more. iTunes is at the core of the iPhone as well, because an iPod is built into the iPhone. You'll employ iTunes to synchronize a bunch of stuff on your computer and iPhone: contacts, calendars, e-mail accounts, bookmarks, photos, videos, and (of course) music.

We get into all that syncing business in Chapter 3.

The Great Escape: Bailing out of your wireless contract

In most instances, a wireless provider will sell you a deeply discounted phone or even issue you a free model. But there's one expensive catch: You're subject to hefty termination fees if you bail out of your (typical) two-year contract early.

The iPhone is one Cingular . . . make that AT&T . . . sensation (bad pun intended), so you'll have to wave sayonara to Sprint, Verizon, or other carriers if you want this device. But breaking a cell phone contract is not easy, and some of the options for doing so may not be quite the outs you had in mind: You can enlist in the military, move overseas, even die. (Sorry, but no guarantee that AT&T's coverage, 3G or otherwise, will reach the heavens.)

Fortunately, there are other strategies, although none are assured of working:

⌐ **Complain loudly and often:** If you've been having problems with your existing carrier, contact the phone company and tell them how lousy your coverage is. Document your complaints in writing and be as specific as possible about spots where your calls drop out.

⌐ **Keep an eye out for price hikes:** If the carrier ups rates dramatically on text messaging, say, you may have a legal out in your contract. The Consumerist.com Web site advises you to read any notices of changes to your Terms of Service that come your way. These may void the original agreement and you'll have about a month to cancel your contract.

⌐ **Use online matchmaking:** Sites such as www.celltradeusa.com and www.cellswapper.com are in the business of matching users who want to get out of their contract with other folks who are seeking a bargain. The person trying to ditch a contract pays a modest fee to these sites. So what's the motivation for the person who takes the contract off your hands? Those who get their phone service this way need not pay an activation fee to the carrier, and they incur no long-term commitment of their own.

⌐ **Roam, roam on the range:** If you keep using your phone outside your carrier's network, it may become uneconomical for *them* to want to keep you. That's because your phone company picks up expensive roaming charges.

Turning the iPhone On and Off

Apple has taken the time to partially charge your iPhone, so you'll get some measure of instant gratification. After taking it out of the box, press and hold the Sleep/Wake button on the top-right edge. (Refer to Chapter 1 for the location of all buttons.) The famous Apple logo should show up on your screen, followed a few seconds later by a stunning image of Earth.

Not so subtle, as messages go: Apple has ambitious aspirations about capturing global market share.

To turn the device completely off, press and hold the Sleep/Wake button again until a red arrow appears at the top of the screen. Then drag the arrow to the right with your finger. Tap Cancel if you change your mind.

Locking the iPhone

Carrying a naked cell phone in your pocket is asking for trouble. Unless the phone has some locking mechanism, you may inadvertently dial a phone number. Try explaining to your boss why he or she got a call from you at 4 a.m. Fortunately, Apple makes it a cinch to lock the iPhone so this scenario won't happen to you.

In fact, you don't need to do anything to lock the iPhone; it happens automatically, as long as you don't touch the screen for a minute.

Can't wait? To lock the iPhone immediately, press the Sleep/Wake button. To unlock it, press the Sleep/Wake button again. Or press the Home button on the front of the screen. Either way, the on-screen slider appears but your iPhone doesn't actually awaken until you drag the slider to the right with your finger.

By now, you're picking up on the idea that your fingers play an instrumental role in controlling your iPhone. We talk more about the responsibility your digits have later in this chapter.

Mastering the Multitouch Interface

Virtually every cell phone known to mankind has a physical (typically plastic) dialing keypad, if not also a more complete QWERTY-style keyboard, to bang out e-mails and text messages. The iPhone dispenses with both. Apple is once again living up to an old company advertising slogan to "Think Different."

Indeed, the iPhone removes the usual physical buttons in favor of a so-called *multitouch display.* It is the heart of many things you do on the iPhone, and the controls change depending on the task at hand.

Unlike other phones with touchscreens, don't bother looking for a stylus. You are meant, instead — at the risk of lifting another ancient ad slogan — to "let your fingers do the walking."

It's important to note that there are actually a half-dozen keyboard layouts in English, all variations on the alphabetical keyboard, the numeric and punctuation keyboard, and the more punctuation and symbols keyboard. These six keyboards are shown in Figure 2-1. The layout you see depends on the application you are working in. For instance, the keyboards in Safari differ from the keyboards in Notes.

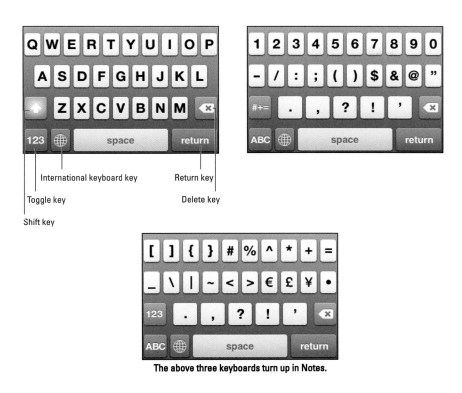

International keyboard key   Return key

Toggle key   Delete key

Shift key

The above three keyboards turn up in Notes.

These three keyboards turn up in Safari.

Figure 2-1: The six faces of the iPhone keyboard.

The iPhone keyboard contains five keys that don't actually type a character: Shift, Toggle, International keyboard, Delete, and Return:

- **Shift key:** If you're using the alphabetical keyboard, the Shift key switches between uppercase and lowercase letters. If you're using either of the other two keyboards, pressing Shift switches to the one you're not currently using.

  To turn on Caps Lock and type in all caps, you first need to enable Caps Lock. You do that by tapping the Settings icon, then tapping General, and then tapping Keyboard. Tap the Enable Caps Lock item to turn it on. Once the Caps Lock setting is enabled (it's disabled by default), you double-tap the Shift key to turn on Caps Lock. (The Shift key turns blue whenever Caps Lock is on.) Tap the Shift key again to turn off Caps Lock. To disable Caps Lock completely, just reverse the process by turning off the Enable Caps Lock setting (tap Settings, General, Keyboard).

- **Toggle key:** Switches between the different keyboard layouts.

- **International keyboard key:** Only shows up if you've turned on an international keyboard, as explained in the sidebar below.

- **Delete key:** Erases the character immediately to the left of the cursor.

  If you hold down the Delete key for a few seconds, it begins erasing entire words rather than individual characters.

- **Return key:** Moves the cursor to the beginning of the next line.

The incredible, intelligent, and virtual iPhone keyboard

Before you consider how to actually *use* the keyboard, we'd like to share a bit of the philosophy behind its so-called *intelligence*. Knowing what makes this keyboard smart will help you make it even smarter when you use it:

- It has a built-in English dictionary that even includes words from today's popular culture.

- It adds your contacts to its dictionary automatically.

- It uses complex analysis algorithms to predict the word you're trying to type.

- It suggests corrections as you type. It then offers you the suggested word just below the misspelled word. When you decline a suggestion and the word you typed is *not* in the iPhone dictionary, the iPhone adds that word to its dictionary and offers it as a suggestion if you mistype the word in the future.

  Remember to decline suggestions (by tapping the characters you typed as opposed to the suggested words that appear beneath what you've typed), as doing so helps your intelligent keyboard become even smarter.

A keyboard for all borders

Apple continues to expand the iPhone's reach globally. English isn't the primary language for many overseas customers, if they speak English at all. Fortunately, Apple doesn't take a parochial approach with iPhone. As part of iPhone 3G and version 2.0 of iPhone software, the company now supplies international keyboard layouts for 21 languages as of this writing. To access a keyboard that isn't customized for Americanized English, tap Settings, General, Keyboard, and International Keyboards — and then flick through the list to select any keyboard you want to use. (Alternatively, tap Settings, General, International, and Keyboard.) Up pops the list shown in the figure included here, with custom keyboards for Korean, German, Japanese, Spanish, Russian, and numerous other languages. Apple even supplies two versions of Portuguese to accommodate customers in Brazil and Portugal, two versions of French (including a keyboard geared to Canadian users), and two versions of Chinese. Heck, there's even a U.K. version of English.

Have a multilingual household? You can select as many of these international keyboards as you might need by tapping the language in the list so that the On button appears in blue. Of course, you can call upon only one at a time. So when you're inside an application that summons a keyboard, tap the little international keyboard button sandwiched between the toggle and space keys (refer back to Figure 2-1) until the keyboard you want to call on for the occasion shows up. Tap again to pick the next keyboard on the corresponding list of international keyboards that you turned on in Settings. If you keep tapping, you come back to your original English keyboard.

One more note about the Chinese keyboards: You can use handwriting character recognition for simplified and traditional Chinese, as shown here. Just drag your finger in the box provided, as shown here. We make apologies in advance for not knowing what the displayed characters here mean (neither one of us speaks Chinese).

✔ It reduces the number of mistakes you make as you type by intelligently and dynamically resizing the touch zones for certain keys. You can't see it, but it is increasing the zones for keys it predicts might come next and decreasing the zones for keys that are unlikely or impossible to come next.

Training your digits

Rice Krispies has Snap! Crackle! Pop! Apple's response for the iPhone is Tap! Flick! and Pinch! Yikes, another ad comparison.

Fortunately, tapping, flicking, and pinching are not challenging gestures, so you'll be mastering many of the iPhone's features in no time:

✔ **Tap:** Tapping serves multiple purposes, as will become evident throughout this book. You can tap an icon to open an application from the Home screen. Tap to start playing a song or to choose the photo album you want to look through. Sometimes you will double-tap (tapping twice in rapid succession), which has the effect of zooming in (or out) of Web pages, maps, and e-mails.

✔ **Flick:** Just what it sounds like. A flick of the finger on the screen itself lets you quickly scroll through lists of songs, e-mails, and picture thumbnails. Tap on the screen to stop scrolling, or merely wait for the scrolling list to stop.

✔ **Pinch/spread:** Place two fingers on the edges of a Web page or picture to enlarge the images or make them smaller. Pinching and spreading (or what we call *un-pinching*) are cool gestures that are easy to master and sure to wow an audience. If you need practice, visit the Apple iPhone blogs at

    www.theiphoneblogs.com/2007/01/12/practice-your-apple-
    iphone-pinch/

The Home screen we discuss back in Chapter 1 may not be the only screen of icons on your phone. After you start adding apps from the iTunes App Store (which you discover in Chapter 14), you may see two or more tiny dots between the Phone, Mail, Safari, and iPod icons and the row of icons directly above them. Those dots denote additional screens, each containing up to 16 additional icons. To navigate between screens, either flick from right to left or left to right across the middle of the screen or tap directly on the dots.

You must be very precise, or you'll open one of the application icons instead of switching screens.

Fingers or thumbs?

There is one last thing: Should you use your fingers or thumbs to type? The answer is: Both. It seems somewhat easier to hold the iPhone in your non-dominant hand (that is, your left hand if you're right-handed or vice versa) and type with the index finger of your dominant hand, especially when you're first starting out with the iPhone. And that's what we suggest you try first.

Later, when you get the hang of typing with one index finger, you can try to speed things up by using both hands. There are two possible ways you can do that:

✔ Set the iPhone on a sturdy surface (such as a desk or table) and tap with both index fingers. Some users prefer this technique. But you can't easily use it when you're standing up with no sturdy surface of the proper height available.

✔ Cup the iPhone with both hands and type with both thumbs. This technique has the advantage of being possible in almost any situation with or without a sturdy surface. The downside is that your thumbs are bigger than your fingers so it takes more practice to type accurately with them — and if you have larger than average thumbs, well, you're flirting with trouble.

Which is better? Don't ask us — try it both ways and use the method that feels the most comfortable or lets you type with the best accuracy. Better still, master both techniques and use whichever is more appropriate at the time.

The number of dots you see represents the current number of screens on your iPhone. The dot that's all white denotes the screen you're currently viewing. Finally, the four icons in the last row — Phone, Mail, Safari, and iPod — are in a special part of the screen known as the *dock*. When you switch from screen to screen as described above, these icons remain on the screen. In other words, only the first 16 icons on the screen change when you move from one screen to another.

Finger-typing

Apple's multitouch interface just might be considered a stroke of genius. And it just might as equally drive you nuts, at least initially.

If you're patient and trusting, you'll get the hang of finger-typing in a week or so. (We've gotten pretty good at it.) You have to rely on the virtual keyboard that appears when you tap a text field to enter notes, compose text messages, type the names of new contacts, and so forth.

Apple's own recommendation — with which we concur — is to start typing with just your index finger before graduating to two thumbs.

As we've already noted, Apple has built a lot of intelligence into its virtual keyboard, so it can correct typing mistakes on the fly and take a stab at predicting what you're about to type next. The keyboard isn't exactly Nostradamus, but it does a pretty good job in coming up with the words you have in mind.

As you press your finger against a letter or number on the screen, the individual key you press gets bigger and practically jumps off the screen, as shown in Figure 2-2. That way, you know that you struck the correct letter or number.

Sending a message to an overseas pal? Keep your finger pressed against a vowel, and a row of keys showing variations on the letter for foreign alphabets pops up, as shown in Figure 2-3. This lets you add the appropriate accent mark. Just slide your finger until the key with the relevant accent mark is pressed.

Meanwhile, if you press and hold the .com key in Safari, it offers you the choice of .com, .net, .edu or .org. Pretty slick stuff.

Alas, mistakes are common at first. Say that you meant to type a sentence in the Notes application that reads, "I am typing a bunch of notes." But because of the way your fingers struck the virtual keys, you actually entered "I am typing a bunch of *npyrs.*" Fortunately, Apple knows that the *o* you meant to press is next to the *p* that showed up on the keyboard, just as *t* and *y* and the *e* and the *r* are side by side. So the software determines that *notes* was indeed the word you had in mind and places it in red under the suspect word, as shown in Figure 2-4. To accept the suggested word, merely tap the Space key. And if for some reason you actually did mean to type *npyrs* instead, tap on the suggested word (*notes* in this example) to decline it.

Figure 2-2: The ABCs of virtual typing.

Figure 2-3: Accenting your letters.

Because Apple knows what you're up to, the virtual keyboard is fine-tuned for the task at hand. If you're entering a Web address, for example, the keyboard inside the Safari Web browser (see Chapter 10) includes dedicated period, forward slash, and .com keys but no Space key. If you're using the Notes application (see Chapter 5), the keyboard does have a Space key. And if you're composing an e-mail message, a dedicated @ key pops up on the keyboard.

When you're typing notes or sending e-mail and want to type a number, symbol, or punctuation mark, you have to tap the *123* key to bring up an alternative virtual keyboard. Tap the *ABC* key to return to the first keyboard. It's not hard to get used to, but some may find this extra step irritating.

See Chapter 18 for a great tip (*Do the Slide for Accuracy and Punctuation*) that demonstrates a slick trick for avoiding the extra step involved in moving between the 123 and ABC keys. The technique takes a bit of practice, but it reduces the irritation and is worth learning sooner rather than later.

Figure 2-4: When the keyboard bails you out.

Editing mistakes

It's a good idea to type with reckless abandon and not get hung up over the characters you mistype. Again, the self-correcting keyboard will fix many errors. That said, plenty of typos will likely turn up, especially in the beginning, and you'll have to make corrections manually.

A neat trick for doing so is to hold your finger against the screen to bring up the magnifying glass shown in Figure 2-5. Use it to position the pointer to the spot where you need to make the correction.

There — you've survived basic training. Now the real fun is about to begin.

Figure 2-5: Magnifying errors.

The Kitchen Sync: Getting Stuff to and from Your iPhone

*W*hen you have passed basic training (in Chapter 2), the next thing you're likely to want to do is get some or all of your contacts, appointments, events, mail settings, bookmarks, ringtones, music, movies, TV shows, podcasts, photos, and applications into your iPhone.

We have good news and . . . more good news. The good news is that you can easily copy any or all of those items from your computer to your iPhone. And the more good news is that once you do that, you can synchronize your contacts, appointments, and events so they're kept up-to-date automatically in both places — on your computer and your iPhone — whenever you make a change in one place or the other. So when you add or change an appointment, an event, or a contact on your iPhone, that information automatically appears on your computer the next time your iPhone and computer communicate.

©iStockphoto.com/ronen

This communication between your iPhone and computer is called *syncing* (short for synchronizing). Don't worry: It's easy, and we're going to walk you through the entire process in this chapter.

But wait. There's even more good news. Items you manage on your computer, such as music, movies, TV shows, podcasts, photos, and e-mail account settings, are synchronized only one way: from your computer to your iPhone, which is the way it should be.

Starting to Sync

Synchronizing your iPhone with your computer is a lot like syncing an iPod with your computer. If you're an iPod user, the process will be a piece of cake. But it's not too difficult even for those who've never used an iPod:

1. **Start by connecting your iPhone to your computer with the USB cable that came with your iPhone.**

   When you connect your iPhone to your computer, iTunes should launch automatically. If it doesn't, chances are you plugged the cable into a USB port on your keyboard, monitor, or hub. Try plugging it into one of the USB ports on your computer instead. Why? Because USB ports on your computer supply more power to a connected device than USB ports on a keyboard, monitor, or most hubs.

   If iTunes still doesn't launch automatically, try launching it manually.

   One last thing: If you've taken any photos with your iPhone since the last time you synced it, your photo-management software (iPhoto on the Mac; Adobe Photoshop Album or Elements on the PC) will launch and ask whether you want to import the photos from your phone. (You find out all about this later in the chapter.)

2. **Select your iPhone in the iTunes source list.**

   You see the Set Up Your iPhone pane, as shown in Figure 3-1. If you've already set up and named your iPhone, you can skip steps 3 and 4a and start with Step 4b.

   If you don't see an iPhone in the source list, and you're sure it's connected to a USB port on your computer (not the keyboard, monitor, or hub), restart your computer.

iPhone selected in source list

Figure 3-1: This is the first thing you see in iTunes.

3. **Name your iPhone.**

   We've named this one *Lisa's iPhone.*

4a. **Decide whether you want iTunes to automatically synchronize your iPhone and your contacts, calendars, e-mail accounts, and bookmarks.**

   - If that's what you want, click the check box next to Automatically Sync Contact, Calendars, Email Accounts, and Bookmarks to make a check mark appear. Then click the Done button and continue with the "Synchronizing Your Media" section later in this chapter.

   - If you want to synchronize manually, make sure the check box is unchecked, as shown in Figure 3-1, and click Done. The "Synchronizing Your Data" section tells you all about how to configure your contacts, calendars, e-mail accounts, and bookmarks manually.

   We've chosen to not select the check box because this computer has four e-mail accounts and we don't want all of them to synchronize with the iPhone.

4b. **After you click the Done button (applies only to those who just performed steps 3 and 4a), the Summary pane should appear. If it doesn't, make sure your iPhone is still selected in the source list and click the Summary tab near the top of the window, as shown in Figure 3-2.**

Figure 3-2: The Summary pane is pretty painless.

5. **If you want iTunes to sync your iPhone automatically whenever you connect it to your computer, click to put a check mark in the Automatically Sync When This iPhone Is Connected check box (in the Options area).**

   Don't select this check box if you want to sync manually by clicking the Sync button at the bottom of the window.

   Your choice in Step 5 is not set in stone. If you select the Automatically Sync When This iPhone Is Connected check box, you can still prevent your iPhone from syncing automatically in several different ways:

   - **Way #1:** After you connect the iPhone to your computer, click the Summary tab in iTunes and uncheck the Automatically Sync When This iPhone Is Connected check box. This prevents iTunes from opening automatically when you connect the iPhone. If you use this method, you can still start a sync manually.

   - **Way #2:** Launch iTunes; then, before you connect your iPhone to your computer, press and hold Command+Option (Mac) or Shift+Ctrl (PC) until you see your iPhone in the iTunes source list. This method prevents your iPhone from syncing automatically just this one time, without changing any settings.

6. **If you want to sync only items that are selected in your iTunes library, select the Only Sync Checked Songs and Videos check box.**

7. **If you want to turn off automatic syncing in the Music and Video panes, check the Manually Manage Music and Videos check box.**

And, of course, if you decide to uncheck the Automatically Sync When This iPhone Is Connected check box, you can always synchronize manually by clicking the Sync button in the bottom-right corner of the window.

By the way, if you've changed any sync settings since the last time you synchronized, the Sync button will instead say Apply.

Disconnecting the iPhone

When the iPhone is syncing with your computer, its screen says *Sync in progress* and iTunes displays a message that says that it's syncing with your iPhone. When the sync is finished, iTunes displays a message that the iPhone sync is complete and it's okay to disconnect your iPhone.

If you disconnect your iPhone before a sync is completed, all or part of the sync may fail.

To cancel a sync so that you can *safely* disconnect your iPhone, drag the slider on the iPhone (the one that says *Slide to Cancel*) during the sync.

If you get a call while you're syncing, the sync is cancelled automatically so that you can safely disconnect your iPhone and answer the call. When you're finished with the call, just reconnect your iPhone to restart the sync.

Synchronizing Your Data

Did you choose to set up data synchronization manually by not selecting the Automatically Sync Contacts, Calendars, Email Accounts, and Bookmarks check box in the Set Up Your iPhone pane shown in Figure 3-1? If you did, your next order of business is to tell iTunes what data you want to synchronize between your iPhone and your computer. You do this by clicking the Info tab, which is to the right of the Summary tab.

The Info pane has six sections: MobileMe, Contacts, Calendars, Mail Accounts, Web Browser, and Advanced. The next sections look at them one by one.

MobileMe

MobileMe is Apple's $99-a-year service for keeping your iPhone, iPod touch, Macs, and PCs synchronized. It is the latest iteration of what Apple used to call .Mac (pronounced dotMac). The big allure of MobileMe is that it can "push" information such as e-mail, calendars, contacts, and bookmarks from your computer to and from your iPhone and keep those items synchronized on your iPhone and computer(s) wirelessly and without human intervention.

If you want to have your e-mail, calendars, contacts, and bookmarks synchronized automatically and wirelessly, click the Set Up Now button. Your Web browser will launch and instructions appear for subscribing to MobileMe if you're not already a subscriber or for setting up each of your devices for MobileMe if you are already a subscriber.

If you're going to use MobileMe to sync your e-mail, calendars, contacts, and bookmarks, you can safely ignore the information in four of the next five sections: Contacts, Calendars, Web Browser, and Advanced. Those four sections deal with using iTunes for synchronization, and you won't need them if you're using MobileMe. You should probably read the fifth section, Mail accounts, even if you're using the MobileMe service for e-mail, because it applies to syncing your mail settings for MobileMe and/or other e-mail accounts.

Contacts

The Contacts section of the Info pane determines how synchronization is handled for your contacts. One method is to synchronize all your contacts, as shown in Figure 3-3. Or you can synchronize any or all groups of contacts you've created in your computer's address-book program; just select the appropriate check boxes in the Selected Groups list, and only those groups will be synchronized.

Figure 3-3: Want to synchronize your contacts? This is where you set things up.

The iPhone syncs with the following address book programs:

- ✓ **Mac:** Address Book and other address books that sync with Address Book, such as Microsoft Entourage
- ✓ **PC:** Windows Address Book (Outlook Express), and Microsoft Outlook
- ✓ **Mac and PC:** Yahoo! Address Book, Google Contacts

On a Mac, you can sync contacts with multiple applications. On a PC, you can sync contacts with only one application at a time.

If you use Yahoo! Address Book, click Configure to enter your Yahoo! ID and password. If you use Google Contacts, click Configure to enter your Google ID and password.

Syncing will never delete a contact from your Yahoo! Address Book if it has a Messenger ID, even if you delete that contact on the iPhone or on your computer.

To delete a contact that has a Messenger ID, log in to your Yahoo! account with a Web browser and delete the contact in your Yahoo! Address Book.

If you sync with your employer's Microsoft Exchange calendar and contacts, all your personal contacts and calendars will be wiped out.

Calendars

The Calendars section of the Info pane determines how synchronization is handled for your appointments and events. You can synchronize all of your calendars, as shown in Figure 3-4. Or you can synchronize any or all individual calendars you've created in your computer's calendar program. Just select the appropriate check boxes.

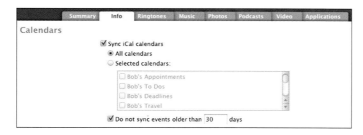

Figure 3-4: Set up sync for your calendar events here.

The iPhone syncs with the following calendar programs:

- ✔ **Mac:** iCal, plus any tasks or events that currently sync with iCal on your Mac, such as events and tasks in Microsoft Entourage
- ✔ **PC:** Microsoft Outlook 2003 or 2007

On a Mac, you can sync calendars with multiple applications. On a PC, you can sync calendars with only one application at a time.

One cool thing about syncing your calendar is that if you create reminders, alerts, or alarms in your computer's calendar program, they appear (and sound) on your iPhone at the appropriate date and time.

Mail accounts

You can sync account settings for your e-mail accounts in the Mail Accounts section of the Info pane. You can synchronize all of your e-mail accounts (if you have more than one), or you can synchronize individual accounts as shown in Figure 3-5. Just select the appropriate check boxes.

The iPhone syncs with the following mail programs:

- ✔ **Mac:** Mail and Microsoft Entourage
- ✔ **PC:** Microsoft Outlook 2003 or 2007 and Microsoft Outlook Express

Figure 3-5: Transfer e-mail account settings to your iPhone here.

E-mail account settings are synchronized only one way: from your computer to your iPhone. If you make changes to any e-mail account settings on your iPhone, the changes will *not* be synchronized back to the e-mail account on your computer. Trust us, this is a very good feature and we're glad Apple did it this way.

By the way, the password for your e-mail account may or may not be saved on your computer. If you sync an e-mail account and the iPhone asks for a password when you send or receive mail, do this: Tap Settings on the Home screen, tap Mail, tap your e-mail account's name, and then type your password in the appropriate field.

Web browser

The Web Browser section has but a single check box, which asks if you want to sync your bookmarks. Select it if you do; don't select it if you don't.

The iPhone syncs bookmarks with the following Web browsers:

- **Mac:** Safari
- **PC:** Microsoft Internet Explorer and Safari

Advanced

Every so often the contacts, calendars, mail accounts, or bookmarks on your iPhone get so screwed up that the easiest way to fix things is to erase that information on your iPhone and replace it with information from your computer.

If that's the case, just click to select the appropriate check boxes, as shown in Figure 3-6. Then the next time you sync, that information on your iPhone will be replaced with information from your computer.

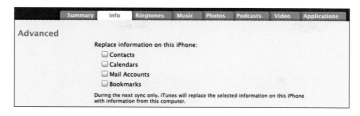

Figure 3-6: Replace the information on your iPhone with the information on your computer.

Because the Advanced section is at the bottom of the Info pane and you have to scroll down to see it, it's easy to forget that it's there. Although you probably won't need to use this feature very often (if ever), you'll be happy you remembered that it's there if you do need it.

Synchronizing Your Media

If you chose to let iTunes manage synchronizing your data automatically, welcome back. This section looks at how you get your media — your ringtones, music, podcasts, video, and photos — from your computer to your iPhone.

Ringtones, music, podcasts, and video (but not photos) are synced only one way: from your computer to your iPhone. Deleting any of these items from your iPhone does not delete them from your computer when you sync.

Ringtones, music, podcasts, and video

You use the Ringtones, Music, Podcasts, and Video panes to specify the media that you want to copy from your computer to your iPhone. To view any of these panes, make sure that your iPhone is still selected in the source list and then click the Music, Podcasts, or Video tab near the top of the window.

Ringtones

If you have any custom ringtones in your iTunes library, select the Sync Ringtones check box. Then you can choose either all ringtones or choose individual ringtones by selecting their check boxes.

Music

To transfer music to your iPhone, select the Sync Music check box in the Music pane. You can then select the button for All Songs and Playlists or

Selected Playlists. If you choose the latter, click the check boxes next to particular playlists you want to transfer. You also can choose to include music videos by selecting the check box at the bottom of the pane (see Figure 3-7.)

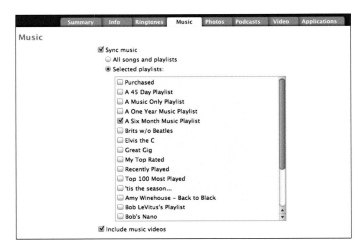

Figure 3-7: Use the Music pane to copy music from your computer to your iPhone.

If you choose All Songs and Playlists and have more songs in your iTunes library than storage space on your iPhone — more than about 7GB on an 8GB iPhone and 14.5GB on a 16GB iPhone — you'll see one or both of the error messages shown in Figure 3-8 when you try to sync.

To avoid these errors, select playlists that total less than 7 or 15 gigabytes.

Music, podcasts, and video are notorious for chewing up massive amounts of storage space on your iPhone.

Figure 3-8: If you have more music than your iPhone has room for, this is what you'll see when you sync.

If you try to sync too much media, you'll see lots of error messages like the ones in Figure 3-8. Forewarned is forearmed.

Podcasts

To transfer podcasts to your iPhone, select the Sync check box in the Podcasts pane. Then you can choose All Podcasts or Selected Podcasts, as shown in Figure 3-9.

Figure 3-9: The Podcasts pane determines which podcasts are copied to your iPhone.

Regardless of whether you choose to sync all podcasts or only selected podcasts, a pop-up menu allows you to specify which episodes you want to sync, as shown in Figure 3-10.

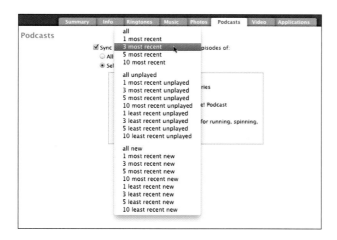

Figure 3-10: This menu determines how podcasts are synced with your iPhone.

Video

To transfer rented movies, TV shows, and movies to your iPhone, select the appropriate check boxes in the Video pane, as shown in Figure 3-11.

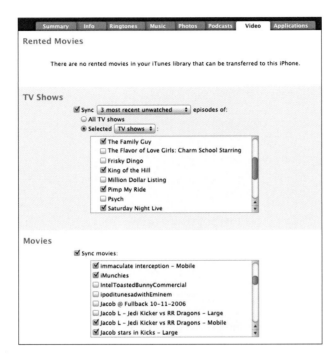

Figure 3-11: Your choices in the Video pane determine which rented movies, TV shows, and movies are copied to your iPhone.

The procedure for syncing TV shows is slightly different from the procedure for syncing movies. First, select the Sync check box to enable TV show syncing. Then choose either All TV Shows or Selected. If you go with Selected, you can then choose between TV Shows and Playlists from the pop-up menu (which says TV Shows in Figure 3-11).

Next, choose how many episodes you want to sync from the pop-up menu shown in Figure 3-12 (which says 3 Most Recent Unwatched).

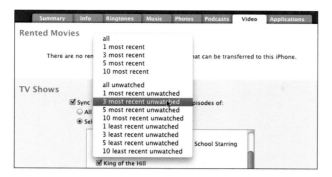

Figure 3-12: This menu determines how TV shows are synced with your iPhone.

To sync rented movies or movies you own, first select the Sync Rented Movies or Sync Movies check box, and then select the check boxes of the individual movies you want to sync.

We don't have any rented movies in our iTunes library, so there's nothing to check in the Rented Movies section in Figure 3-11 or Figure 3-12. Rest assured that if we *did* have rented movies, they would definitely appear right there in the Rented Movies section.

Photos

Syncing photos is a little different from syncing other media because your iPhone has a built-in camera and you may want to copy pictures you take with the iPhone to your computer, as well as copy pictures stored on your computer to your iPhone.

The iPhone syncs photos with the following programs:

- ✓ **Mac:** iPhoto version 4.03 or later, Aperture, and any folder that contains images
- ✓ **PC:** Adobe Photoshop Album 2.0 or later, Adobe Photoshop Elements 3.0 or later

You can also sync photos with any folder on your computer that contains images.

To sync photos, click the Photos tab near the top of the window. In the Photos pane, select the Sync Photos From check box and then choose an application or folder from the pop-up menu (which says iPhoto in Figure 3-13).

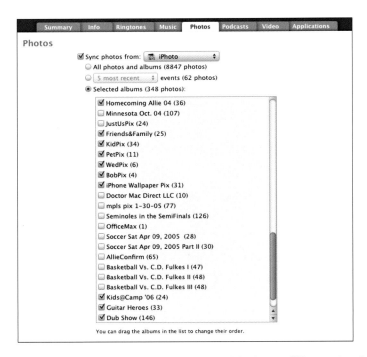

Figure 3-13: The Photos pane determines which photos will be synchronized with your iPhone.

If you choose an application that supports photo albums, as in Figure 3-13 by choosing iPhoto, you can then select specific albums to sync. If you choose a folder full of images, you can create subfolders inside it which will appear as albums on your iPhone. But if you choose an application that doesn't support albums, or a single folder full of images with no subfolders, you have to transfer all or nothing.

Because we selected iPhoto in the Sync Photos From menu, and iPhoto '08 (the version installed on our Mac) supports Events in addition to albums, we have the option of syncing events instead of albums if we prefer.

If you have lots of albums or events, you can rearrange the list so that the ones you expect to check or uncheck most often are near the top. Simply click an album or event name and drag it up or down in the list.

If you've taken any photos with your iPhone since the last time you synced it, the appropriate program will launch (or the appropriate folder will be selected), and you'll have the option of downloading the pictures to your computer. The process is the same as when you download pictures from your digital camera.

Applications

If you have downloaded or purchased any iPhone applications from the iTunes App Store, click the Applications tab and then select the Sync Applications check box. Then you can choose either All Applications or choose individual applications by selecting their check boxes.

How much space did I use?

If you're interested in knowing how much free space is available on your iPhone, look near the bottom of the iTunes window while your iPhone is selected in the source list. You'll see a chart that shows the contents of your iPhone, color-coded for your convenience. As you can see in Figure 3-14, this 16GB iPhone has roughly 1.53GB of free space available.

Capacity	Audio	Video	Photos	Other	Free Space
14.64 GB	8.32 GB	4.38 GB	96.8 MB	333 MB	1.53 GB

Figure 3-14: This handy chart shows you how much space is being used on your iPhone.

The chart appears at the bottom of the iTunes window, regardless of which pane is currently selected.

Here's a cool trick: Click directly on the chart and watch the units of measure switch from gigabytes/megabytes to songs/items/photos and days/hours.

In case you're wondering, Other is the catch-all category for contacts, calendars, appointments, events, bookmarks, applications, and e-mail stored on your phone. In our case, the total of these items is a mere 333MB, a tiny fraction of the total storage space available on this iPhone.

Part II
The Mobile iPhone

The 5th Wave — By Rich Tennant

"Of course your iPhone lets you watch videos, listen to music, and surf the Web. But does it shoot silly string?"

*Y*our iPhone is first and foremost a mobile phone, so in this part we explore how to use typical mobile phone features, starting with all the neat ways to make an outgoing phone call. You also find out how to answer or ignore the calls that come in and discover iPhone's clever visual voicemail feature, which lets you take in messages on your terms, rather than in the order in which the messages arrived on the phone. You also figure out how to juggle calls, merge calls, and decide on a ringtone.

After you've mastered all the calling and listening stuff, you are ready to become a whiz at sending and retrieving what are called SMS text messages. As journalists, we especially appreciate what comes next: finding out how to become a champion note-taker.

We close this part by investigating all those C-word programs — namely, Calendar, Calculator, and Clock. These handy applications not only enable you to solve arithmetic problems on the fly (with one or two nifty calculators), but they also help you stay on top of your appointments and — thanks to a built-in alarm clock — show up for them on time.

Understanding the Phone-damentals

You may well have bought an iPhone for its spectacular photo viewer, marvelous widescreen iPod, and the best darn pocket-sized Internet browser you've ever come across. Not to mention its overall coolness.

For most of us, though, cool goes only so far. The iPhone's most critical mission is the one from which its name is derived — it is first and foremost a cell phone. And no matter how capable it is at all those other things, when push comes to shove you had best be able to make and receive phone calls.

That puts a lot of responsibility in the hands of AT&T, the iPhone's exclusive wireless carrier in the U.S. As with any cell phone, the strength of the wireless signal depends a great deal on your location and the robustness of the carrier's network.

©iStockphoto.com/kledge

As noted in Chapter 1, the cell-signal status icon at the upper-left corner of the screen can clue you in on what your phone-calling experience may be like. Simply put, more bars supposedly equate to a better experience. What you hope to avoid are those two dreaded words . . . *No Service*.

Cell coverage aside, this chapter is devoted to all the nifty ways you can handle wireless calls on an iPhone.

Somewhere Alexander Graham Bell is beaming.

Making a Call

Start by tapping the Phone icon on the Home screen. You can then make calls by tapping any of the icons that show up at the bottom of the screen: Contacts, Favorites, Recents, Keypad, or Voicemail. Depending on the circumstances, one of these could be the most appropriate method. Let's take them one by one.

Contacts

If you read the chapter on syncing (Chapter 3), you know how to get the snail-mail addresses, e-mail addresses, and (most relevant for this chapter) phone numbers that reside on your PC or Mac into the iPhone. Assuming that you went through that drill already, all those addresses and phone numbers are hanging out in one place. Their not-so-secret hiding place is revealed when you tap the Contacts icon inside the Phone application or the Contacts icon on one of the Home screen pages.

Here's how to make those contacts work to your benefit:

1. **Inside the Phone application, tap Contacts.**

2. **Flick your finger so the list of contacts on the screen scrolls rapidly up or down, loosely reminiscent of the spinning Lucky 7s (or other pictures) on a Las Vegas slot machine.**

   Think of the payout you'd get with that kind of power on a One-Armed Bandit.

   Alternatively, you can move your fingers along the alphabet on the right edge of the Contacts list or tap one of the teeny-tiny letters that make up that alphabet to jump to names that begin with that letter.

   As part of the 2.0 software upgrade for iPhone, you also can find a list of potential matches by starting to type the name of a contact in the new search field near the top of the list. Or you can type the name of the place your contact works. You may have to flick to get the search field into view.

3. **When you're at or near the appropriate contact name, stop the scrolling by tapping the screen.**

   Note that when you tap to stop the scrolling, that tap doesn't select an item in the list. That may seem counterintuitive the first few times you try it, but we got used to it and now we really like it this way.

Tap the status bar to automatically scroll to the top of the list. This is useful if you're really popular (or influential) and have a whole bunch of names among your contacts.

4. **Tap the name of the person you want to call.**

As shown in Figure 4-1, you can see a bunch of fields with the individual's phone numbers, physical and e-mail addresses, and possibly even a mug shot.

Odds are pretty good that the person has more than one phone number, so the hardest decision you must make is choosing which of these to call.

5. **Tap the phone number, and the iPhone initiates the call.**

If you lumped your contacts into Groups on your computer, reflecting, say, different departments in your company or friends from work, friends from school, and so on, you can tap the Groups button on the upper-left side of the All Contacts screen to access these groups.

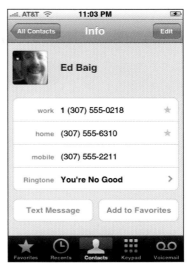

Figure 4-1: Contact me.

Your own iPhone phone number, lest you forget it, appears at the top of the Contacts list, provided you arrived in Contacts through the Phone application.

You can also initiate text messages and e-mails from within Contacts. Those topics are discussed in greater depth in Chapters 5 and 11, respectively.

Favorites

Consider Favorites the iPhone equivalent of speed-dialing. It's where you can keep a list of the people and numbers you dial most often. Merely tap the person's name in Favorites and your iPhone calls the person.

You can set up as many favorites as you need for a person. So, for example, you may create separate Favorites listings for both your spouse's office phone number and cell number.

Setting up Favorites is a breeze. When looking at one of your contacts, you may have noticed the Add to Favorites button. When you tap this button, all the phone numbers you have for that person pop up. Tap the number you want to make into a favorite and it turns up on the list.

You can rearrange the order in which your favorites are displayed. Tap Edit, and then, to the right of the person you want to move, press your finger against the symbol that looks like three short horizontal lines stacked on top of one another. Drag that symbol to the place on the list where you want your favorite contact to appear.

You can designate new favorites from within the Favorites application by tapping the + symbol at the upper-right corner of the screen. Doing so brings you back to Contacts. From there, choose the appropriate person and number. A star appears next to any contact's number picked as a favorite.

If any of your chosen folks happen to fall out of favor, you can easily kick them off the Favorites roster. Here's how:

1. **Tap the Edit button in the upper-left corner of the screen.**

   You'll notice that a red circle with a horizontal white line appears to the left of each name in the list.

2. **Tap the circle next to the A-lister getting the heave-ho.**

   The horizontal white line is now vertical and a red Remove button appears to the right of the name, as shown in Figure 4-2.

3. **Tap Remove.**

   The person (or one of his or her given phone numbers) is no longer afforded the privilege of being in your iPhone inner circle.

Booting someone off the Favorites list does not remove that person from the main Contacts list.

Figure 4-2: I don't like you as much anymore.

Recents

Tapping the Recents icon displays the iPhone call log. The Recents feature houses logs of all the, well, *recent* calls made or received, as well as calls that you missed. Here's a tricky concept: Tap All to show all the recent calls and Missed to show just those you missed. Under the All list, completed calls are shown in black and missed calls are in red.

By tapping the small blue circle with the right-pointing arrow next to an item in the list, you can access information about the time a call was made or missed, as well as any known information about the caller from your Contacts information.

To return a call, just tap anywhere on the name.

If one of the calls you missed came from someone who isn't already in your Contacts, you can add him or her. Tap the right-pointing arrow, and then tap the Create New Contact button.

If the person is among your Contacts but has a new number, tap the Add to Existing Contact button.

When the list gets too long, tap Clear to clean it up.

Keypad

From time to time, of course, you have to dial the number of a person or company who hasn't earned a spot in your Contacts.

That's when you'll want to tap the keypad icon to bring up the large keys of the virtual touch-tone keypad you see in Figure 4-3. Despite what you may have read elsewhere, we find it surprisingly simple to manually dial a number on this keypad. Just tap the appropriate keys and tap Call.

To add this number to your address book, tap the + key (it's the one with the silhouette) on the keypad and click either Create New Contact or Add to Existing Contact.

Quibble: You won't be able to dial without looking at the screen; dialing without looking is possible on at least some of the handsets with physical keypads. Moreover, at least until some third party apps came along, you couldn't dial Phone by voice either. Voice dialing on some phones lets you call Mom simply by saying out loud, "Call Mom."

Figure 4-3: A virtually familiar way to dial.

You can use the iPhone's keypad also to remotely check your voicemail at work or home.

Come to think of it, what a perfect segue into the next section. It's on one of our favorite iPhone features, visual voicemail.

Visual voicemail

How often have you had to listen to four or five (or more) voicemail messages before getting to the message you really want, or need, to hear? As shown in Figure 4-4, the iPhone's clever visual voicemail presents a list of your voicemail messages in the order in which calls were received. But you need not listen to those messages in order.

How do you even know you have voicemail? There are a few ways:

Blue dot

Playhead

Scrubber bar

Home button

Figure 4-4: Visual voicemail in action.

- ✔ A red circle showing the number of pending messages awaiting your attention appears above the Phone icon on the Home screen, or above the Voicemail icon from within the Phone application.

- ✔ You may also see a message on the iPhone display that says something like, "New voicemail from Ed (or Bob)."

Whatever draws you in, tap that Voicemail icon to display the list of voicemails. You see the caller's phone number, assuming this info is known through CallerID, and in some cases, his or her name. Or you see the word *Unknown*.

The beauty of all this, of course, is that you can ignore (or at least put off listening to) certain messages. We are not in the advice-giving business on what calls you can safely avoid; if you ignore messages from the IRS or your parole officer, it's at your own risk, okay?

The globetrotting iPhone

Apple has managed to cram ten radios into the latest iPhone. It's got four *GSM/Edge* radios *(850, 900, 1800, 1900 MHz),* three *UMTS/HSDPA* radios, plus radios for Bluetooth, Wi-Fi, and GPS. And here's a little bit of trivia: The metal ring around the iPhone camera is part of the antenna design.

Before you break into a sweat over the terminology, know that all we're really talking about is a 3G or "third-generation" phone you can use to make calls (and do more) while traveling abroad. You'll have to have AT&T turn on something called *international roaming* (unless, of course, you live in a foreign land and have a local carrier). Contact AT&T for the latest rates, which were fairly harsh at the time this book

was being prepared. Go to `www.wireless.att.com/learn/international` for details.

If you're calling the U.S. while overseas, you can take advantage of International Assist. It's a feature that automatically adds the proper prefix to U.S. numbers dialed from abroad. Tap Settings, Phone, and then International Assist. Make sure you see the blue On button instead of the white Off button.

Although iPhone started out as a U.S.-only proposition, Apple launched versions of the iPhone in nearly two dozen countries in the summer of 2008, with at least 70 in all planned by the end of the calendar year.

A blue dot next to a name or number signifies that you haven't heard the message yet.

To play back a voicemail, tap the name or number in question. Then tap the tiny Play/Pause button that shows up to the left. Tap once more to pause the message; tap again to resume. Tap the Speaker button if you want to hear the message through the iPhone's speakerphone.

Tap the blue arrow next to a caller's name or number to bring up any contact info on the person or to add the caller to your Contacts.

The tiny playhead along the Scrubber bar (refer to Figure 4-4) shows you the length of the message and how much of the message you've heard. If you hate when callers ramble on forever, you can drag the playhead to rapidly advance through a message. Perhaps more importantly, if you miss something, you can replay that segment.

Returning a call is as simple as tapping the green Call Back button. And you can delete a voicemail by pressing Delete.

If you have no phone service, you'll see a message that says *Visual Voicemail is currently unavailable.*

You can listen to your iPhone voicemail from another phone. Just dial your iPhone number and, while the greeting plays, enter your voicemail password. You can set up such a password by tapping Settings from the Home screen and then tapping Phone. Tap Change Voicemail Password. You'll be asked to enter your current voicemail password, if you already have one. If one doesn't exist yet, tap Done. If it does exist, enter it and then tap Done. You'll then be asked to type the new password and tap Done, twice.

Recording a greeting

You have two choices when it comes to the voicemail greeting your callers will hear. You can accept a generic greeting with your phone number by default. Or you can create a custom greeting in your own voice. The steps:

1. **Inside the voicemail application, tap the Greeting button.**

2. **Tap Custom.**

3. **Tap Record and start dictating a clever, deserving-of-being-on-the-iPhone voicemail greeting.**

4. **When you have finished recording, tap Stop.**

5. **Review the greeting by pressing Play.**

6. **If the greeting is worthy, tap Save. If not, tap Cancel and start over at Step 1.**

Receiving a Call

It's wonderful to have numerous options for making a call. But what are your choices when somebody calls you? The answer depends on whether you are willing to take the call or not.

Accepting the call

To accept a call, you have three options:

- Tap Answer and greet the caller in whatever language makes sense.

- If the phone is locked, drag the slider to the right.

- If you are donning the stereo earbuds that come with the iPhone, click the microphone button.

Actually, you have a fourth option if you wear a wireless Bluetooth headset or use a car speakerphone. Click the Answer button on your headset or speakerphone (refer to the manual if the process isn't intuitive). For more on Bluetooth, read Chapter 13.

If you are listening to music in your iPhone's iPod when a call comes in, the song stops playing and you have to decide whether to take the call. If you do, the music resumes from where you left off once the conversation ends.

Rejecting the call

We're going to assume that you're not a cold-hearted person out to break a caller's heart. Rather, we assume that you are a busy person who will call back at a more convenient time.

Keeping that positive spin in mind, here are three ways to reject a call on the spot and send the call to voicemail:

- Tap Decline. Couldn't be easier than that.
- Press the Sleep/Wake button twice in rapid succession. (The button is on the top of the device.)
- Using the supplied headset, press and hold the Microphone button for a couple of seconds and then let go. Two beeps let you know that the call was indeed rejected.

Sometimes you're perfectly willing to take a call but you need to silence the ringer or turn off the vibration. To do so, press the Sleep/Wake button a single time, or press one of the volume buttons. You'll still have the opportunity to answer.

Choosing ringtones

At the time this book was written, Apple included 25 ringtones in the iPhone, ranging from the sound of crickets to an old car horn. Read the "iTunes and ringtones" sidebar to figure out how to create your own custom ringtones.

To choose a ringtone, follow these steps:

1. **From the Home screen, tap Settings.**
2. **Tap Sounds.**
3. **Tap Ringtone to access the list of available ringtones, shown in Figure 4-5.**
4. **Flick your finger to move up or down the list.**

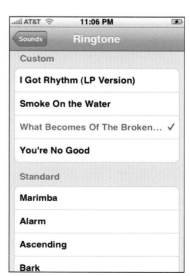

Figure 4-5: Ring my chimes: The iPhone's ringtones.

5. **Tap any of the ringtones to hear what it will sound like.**

   A check mark appears next to the ringtone you've just listened to. If need be, adjust the volume slider in Sounds.

6. **If satisfied, you need do nothing more. Unbeknownst to you, you have just selected that ringtone. If not pleased, try another.**

TIP

You can easily assign specific ringtones to individual callers. From Contacts, choose the person to whom you want to designate a particular ringtone. Tap Edit and then tap Assign Ringtone. This displays the aforementioned list of ringtones. Choose the one that seems most appropriate (a barking dog, say, for your father-in-law).

To change or delete the ringtone for a specific person, go back into Contacts, and tap Edit. Either tap the right arrow to choose a new ringtone for that person or tap the red circle and Delete to remove the custom ringtone altogether.

iTunes and ringtones

When Apple first launched iPhone in June 2007, we were disappointed that we couldn't use snippets of music from our iTunes library for ringtones. It took a couple of months, but iPhone owners can now turn some of the songs they've purchased (or will buy) into custom ringtones. You must fork over 99 cents for songs that are already in your iTunes library on your computer or pay $1.98 for a new song from the iTunes Store online (which lets you also get full use of the track on your PC or Mac.)

The ringtone-ready music in your own iTunes collection is designated by a little bell symbol. Clicking that symbol brings up a ringtone editor that resembles Apple's GarageBand music editing software. Drag the editor over the portion of the song you want to use as your ringtone — up to 30 seconds worth. You can choose to have the ringtone fade in or out by checking the appropriate boxes in the editor. Click Preview to make sure that you're happy with the result, and click Buy when you're satisfied.

Connect the iPhone to your computer to synchronize the ringtone.

Actually, you can also create custom ringtones in GarageBand and through such third-party utilities as iToner. Head to Chapter 18 for more details on GarageBand ringtoning. (We love coining new verbs).

While on a Call

You can do lots of things while talking on an iPhone, such as consulting your Calendar, taking notes, or checking the weather. Tap the Home button to get to these other applications. You've just witnessed the multitasking marvel that is the iPhone.

If you're using Wi-Fi or 3G, you can also surf the Web (through Safari) while talking on the phone. But you can't surf while you talk if your only outlet to cyberspace is the EDGE network.

Other options:

Figure 4-6: Managing calls.

- **Mute a call:** From the main call screen (shown in Figure 4-6) tap Mute. Now you need not mutter under your breath when a caller ticks you off; the caller can't hear you. Tap Mute again to un-mute the sound.

- **Tap Contacts to display the Contacts list.**

- **Place a call on hold:** Again, pretty self-explanatory. Just tap Hold. Tap Hold again to take the person off hold. You might put a caller on hold to answer another incoming call or to make a second call yourself. The next section deals with more than one call at a time.

- **Tap Keypad to bring back the keypad:** This is useful if you have to type touch-tones to access another voicemail system or respond to an automated menu system. Heaven forbid you actually get a live person when calling an insurance company or airline. But we digress. . . .

- **Use the speakerphone:** Tap Speaker to listen to a call through the iPhone's internal speakers without having to hold the device up to your mouth.

- **Make a conference call:** Read on.

Juggling calls

You can field a new call when you're already talking to somebody. Or ignore it (by tapping Ignore).

To take the new call while keeping the first caller on hold, tap the Hold Call + Answer button that appears, as shown in Figure 4-7. You can then toggle between calls (placing one or the other on hold) by tapping either the Swap button or the first call at the top of the screen.

If this is too much for you and that second caller is really important, tap End Call + Answer to ditch caller number one.

Conference calls

Figure 4-7: Swapping calls.

Now suppose caller number one and caller number two know each other. Or you'd like to play matchmaker so they get to know each other. Tap Merge Calls so all three of you can chitchat. At first the phone number of each caller will scroll at the top of your screen like a rolling ticker. A few seconds later the ticker is replaced by the word *Conference* with a circled right-pointing arrow to its immediate right.

Now let's assume you have to talk to your whole sales team at once. It may be time to initiate a full-blown conference call, which effectively takes this merge-call idea to its extreme. You can merge up to five calls at a time. In fact, creating such a conference call on the iPhone may be simpler than getting the same five people in a physical room at the same time.

Here's how you do it. Start by making a call and then placing the caller on hold as noted earlier in the "Juggling calls" section. Tap Add Call to make another call and then Merge Calls to bring everybody together. Repeat this exercise to add the other calls.

Other conference call tidbits:

- iPhone is actually a two-line phone, and one of the available lines can be involved in a conference call.

- If you want to drop a call from a conference, tap Conference and then tap the red circle with the little picture of the phone in it that appears next to the call. Tap End Call to make that caller go bye-bye.

✓ You can speak privately with one of the callers in a conference. Tap Conference, and then tap Private next to the caller you want to go hush-hush with. Tap Merge Calls to bring the caller back into the Conference so everyone can hear him or her.

✓ You can add a new incoming caller to an existing conference call by tapping Hold Call + Answer followed by Merge Calls.

There's even more you can do with iPhone the phone. Check out Chapter 13 for extra phone tips. Meanwhile, we recommend that you read the next chapter to figure out how to become a whiz at text messaging.

Texting 1, 2, 3:
SMS Messages and Notes

*T*here has never been a device like the iPhone, so chances are this is your first experience with an intelligent virtual keyboard. In the beginning, it will probably feel awkward. Within a few days, however, many iPhone users report that they not only have become comfortable using it but have become proficient virtual typists as well.

By the time you finish this chapter, we think you'll feel comfortable and proficient, too. You discover all about using the virtual keyboard in Chapter 2. In this chapter, we focus on two of the iPhone applications that use text — namely Text (SMS) and Notes.

Texting

The Text application lets you exchange short text messages with any cell phone that supports the SMS protocol (which is almost all cell phones today).

SMS is the acronym for the Short Message Service protocol, often known as *text messaging* or just plain *texting*.

©iStockphoto.com/kutay tanir

Typing text on a cell phone with a 12-key numeric keypad is an unnatural act, which is why many people have never sent a single SMS text message. The iPhone will change that. The intelligent virtual keyboard makes it easy to compose short text messages, and the big, bright, high-resolution screen makes it a pleasure to read them.

But before we get to the part where you send or receive SMS messages, let's go over some SMS basics:

- **Both sender and receiver need SMS-enabled mobile phones.** Your iPhone qualifies, as does almost any mobile phone made in the past four or five years. Keep in mind that if you send SMS messages to folks with a phone that doesn't support SMS, they will never get your message nor will they even know you sent a message.

- **Some phones (not the iPhone, of course) limit SMS messages to 160 characters.** If you try to send a longer message to one of these phones, your message may be truncated or split into multiple shorter messages. The point is that it's a good idea to keep SMS messages brief.

- **AT&T iPhone plans no longer include SMS text messages.** Individual SMS text messages cost 20¢ each unless you subscribe to one of the optional SMS text message plans, which start at $5 per month for 200 messages.

    Each individual message in a conversation counts against this total, even if it's only a one-word reply such as "OK," or "CUL8R" (which is Teenager for "see you later").

- **You can increase the number of SMS messages in your plan for a few more dollars a month.** This is almost always less expensive than paying for them à la carte.

- **You can send or receive SMS messages only over your wireless carrier's network (which is AT&T in the U.S.).** In other words, SMS messages can't be sent or received over a Wi-Fi connection.

Okay, now that we have that out of the way, let's start with how to send SMS text messages.

You send me: Sending SMS text messages

Tap the Text (SMS) icon on the Home screen to launch the Text application, and then tap the little pencil-and-paper icon in the top-right corner of the screen to start a new text message.

 At this point, the To field is active and awaiting your input. You can do three things at this point:

- If the recipient isn't in your Contacts list, type his or her cell-phone number.

- If the recipient *is* in your Contacts list, type the first few letters of the name. A list of matching contacts appears. Scroll through it if necessary and tap the name of the contact.

    The more letters you type, the shorter the list becomes.

✔ Tap the blue plus icon on the right side of the To field to select a name from your Contacts list.

There's a fourth option if you want to compose the message first and address it later. Tap inside the text-entry field (the oval-shaped area just above the keyboard and to the left of the Send button) to activate it, and then type your message. When you've finished typing, tap the To field and use one of the preceding techniques to address your message.

When you have finished addressing and composing, tap the Send button to send your message on its merry way. And that's all there is to it.

Being a golden receiver: Receiving SMS text messages

First things first. If you want to hear an alert sound when you receive an SMS text message, tap the Settings icon on your Home screen, tap Sounds, tap the New Text Message item, and then tap one of the available sounds. You can audition the sounds by tapping them.

You hear the sounds when you audition them in the Settings app, even if you have the Ring/Silent switch set to Silent. After you exit the Settings application, however, you *won't* hear a sound when an SMS message arrives if the Ring/Silent switch is set to Silent.

If you *don't* want to hear an alert when an SMS message arrives, instead of tapping one of the listed sounds, tap the first item in the list: None.

If you receive an SMS text message when your phone is asleep, all or part of the text message and the name of the sender appear on the Unlock screen when you wake your phone.

If your phone is awake and unlocked when an SMS text message arrives, all or part of the message and the name of the sender appear on the screen in front of whatever's already there, along with Close and Reply buttons. At the same time, the Text icon on the Home screen displays the number of unread messages. You can see all of this in Figure 5-1.

Number of new messages

Sender's name   Message

Figure 5-1: What you see if your iPhone is awake when an SMS text message arrives.

To read or reply to the message, tap Reply.

To read or reply to a message after you've tapped the Close button, tap the Text icon. If a message other than the one you're interested in appears on the screen when you launch the Text application, tap Messages in the top-left corner of the screen, and then tap the recipient's name; that person's messages appear on the screen.

To reply to the message on the screen, tap the text-entry field to the left of the Send button, and the keyboard appears. Type your reply and then tap Send.

Your conversation is saved as a series of text bubbles. Your messages appear on the right side of the screen in green bubbles; the other person's messages appear on the left in gray bubbles, as shown in Figure 5-2.

You can delete a conversation in two ways:

✒ **If you're viewing the conversation:** Tap the Clear button at the top right of the conversation screen.

✒ **If you're viewing the list of text messages:** Tap the Edit button at the top left of the Text Messages list, tap the red minus icon that appears to the left of the person's name, and then tap the Delete button that appears to the right of the name.

What you said

What they said

Figure 5-2: This is what an SMS conversation looks like.

Smart SMS tricks

Here are some more things you can do with SMS text messages:

✒ To send an SMS text message to someone in your Favorites or Recents list, tap the Phone icon on the Home screen, and then tap Favorites or Recents, respectively. Tap the blue > icon to the right of a name or number, and then scroll down and tap Text Message at the bottom of the Info screen.

✔ To call or e-mail someone to whom you've sent an SMS text message, tap the Text icon on the Home screen, and then tap the person's name in the Text Messages list. Tap the Call button at the top of the conversation to call the person, or tap the Contact Info button and then tap an e-mail address to send an e-mail.

You can use this technique only if the contact has an e-mail address.

✔ To add someone to whom you've sent an SMS text message to your Contacts list, tap the person's name or phone number in the Text Messages list and then tap the Add to Contacts button.

✔ If an SMS message includes a URL, tap it to open that Web page in Safari.

✔ If an SMS message includes a phone number, tap it to call that number.

✔ If an SMS message includes an e-mail address, tap it to open a pre-addressed e-mail message in Mail.

✔ If an SMS message includes a street address, tap it to see a map in Maps.

And that's all there is to it. You are now an official SMS text-message maven.

Take Note of Notes

Notes is an application that creates text notes that you can save or send through e-mail. To create a note, first tap the Notes icon on the Home screen, and then tap the plus button in the top-right corner to start a new note. The virtual keyboard appears. Type the note. When you're finished, tap the Done button in the top-right corner to save the note, as shown in Figure 5-3. (The Done button only appears when the virtual keyboard is on-screen, however, so you can't see it in the figure.)

After a note is saved, you can do the following:

✔ Tap the Notes button at the top-left corner of the screen to see a list of all your notes. When the list is on-screen, just tap a note to open and view it.

✔ Tap the left or right arrow button at the bottom of the screen to read the previous or next note.

Figure 5-3: The Notes application revealed.

✔ Tap the letter icon at the bottom of the screen to e-mail the note using the Mail application (see Chapter 11 for more about Mail).

✔ Tap the trash can icon at the bottom of the screen to delete the note.

And that's all there is to it. You now know everything there is to know about creating and managing notes with Notes.

Calendars, and Calculators, and Clocks, Oh My

> ## In This Chapter
> ▷ Understanding the calendar's different views and functions
> ▷ Calculating with your iPhone
> ▷ Using the clock as an alarm, a stopwatch, and a timer too

*T*he iPhone is a smartphone. And as a smart device it can remind you of appointments, tell you the time where you live (or halfway around the world), and even solve simple arithmetic.

Over the next few pages we look at three of the iPhone's core — if frankly unsexy — applications. Indeed, we'd venture to say none of you actually bought an iPhone because of its calendar, calculator, or clock. Just the same, it's awfully handy having these programs around.

Working with the Calendar

The Calendar program lets you keep on top of your appointments and events (birthdays, anniversaries, and the like). You get there by tapping the Calendar icon on the Home screen. The icon is pretty smart in its own right because it changes daily; the day of the week and date are displayed.

©iStockphoto.com/narvikk

You have three main ways to peek at your calendar: List, Day, and Month views. Choosing one is as simple as tapping on the List, Day, or Month button at the bottom of the Calendar screen. From each view, you can always return to the current day by tapping the Today button.

A closer look. . . .

List view

Nothing complicated with the List view. As the name indicates, the List view, shown in Figure 6-1, presents current and future appointments in a list format. You can drag the list up or down with your finger. Or flick to rapidly scroll through the list. The List view pretty much compensates for the lack of a week-at-a-glance view, though Apple certainly could add such a feature, perhaps even by the time you read this book.

If you're a Mac user who uses iCal, you can create multiple calendars and choose which ones to sync with your phone (as described in Chapter 3). What's more, you can choose to display any or all of your calendars.

The iPhone can display the color-coding you assigned in iCal. Cool, huh?

But be careful: To-do items created in iCal are not synced and won't appear on your iPhone.

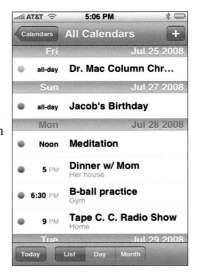

Figure 6-1: The List view.

Day view

The Day view, shown in Figure 6-2, reveals the appointments of a given 24-hour period (though you'll have to scroll up or down to see an entire day's worth of entries).

Month view

By now you're getting the hang of this. In Month view you can see appointments from January to December. In this monthly calendar view, you see a dot on any day that has appointments or events. Tap that day to see the list of activities that the dot represents. It's just below the month in view, as shown in Figure 6-3.

Figure 6-2: The Day view.

Figure 6-3: The Month view.

Adding Calendar Entries

In Chapter 3 you discover pretty much everything there is to know about syncing your
iPhone. And that includes syncing calendar
entries from your Windows machine (via the
likes of Microsoft Outlook) or Mac (via iCal or
Microsoft Entourage).

Of course, in plenty of situations you'll want to
enter appointments on-the-fly. It's very easy to
add appointments directly to the iPhone:

1. **Tap the Calendar icon at the top of the
   screen, and then tap the List, Day, or
   Month button.**

2. **Tap the + button at the upper-right
   corner of the screen.**

   The + appears whether you are in
   List, Day, or Month view. Tapping +
   displays the Add Event screen, shown
   in Figure 6-4.

Figure 6-4: You are about to add an
event to your iPhone.

3. **Tap the Title/Location field and finger-type as much (or as little) information as you feel is necessary.**

   Tapping displays the virtual keyboard.

4. **Tap Save.**

5. **If your calendar entry has a start time or end time (or both):**

   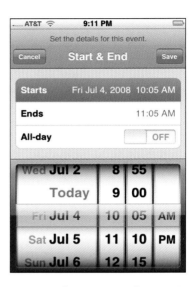

   Figure 6-5: Controlling the Starts and Ends fields is like manipulating a bike lock.

   a. Tap the Starts/Ends field.

   b. In the bottom half of the screen that appears (see Figure 6-5), choose the time the event starts and then the time it ends.

   Use your finger to roll separate wheels for the date, hour, minute (in 5-minute intervals), and to specify AM or PM. It's a little like manipulating one of those combination bicycle locks or an old-fashioned date stamp used with an inkpad.

   c. Tap Save when you're finished.

6. **If you are entering a birthday or another all-day milestone, tap the All-day button so that On (rather than Off) is showing. Then tap Save.**

Since the time isn't relevant for an all-day entry, you'll note that the bottom half of the screen now has wheels for just the month, day, and year.

7. **If you are setting up a recurring entry, such as an anniversary, tap the Repeat window. Tap to indicate how often the event in question recurs, and then tap Save.**

   The options are Every Day, Every Week, Every 2 Weeks, Every Month, and Every Year.

8. **If you want to set a reminder or alert for the entry, tap Alert. Then tap on a time, and then tap Save.**

   Figure 6-6: Alerts make it hard to forget.

   Alerts can be set to arrive on the actual date of an event, 2 days before, 1 day before, 2 hours before, 1 hour before, 30 minutes before, 15 minutes before, or 5 minutes before. At Alert time, you'll hear a sound and see a message like the one shown in Figure 6-6.

Are you the kind of person who needs an extra nudge? You can set another reminder by tapping on the Second Alert field.

9. **Tap Calendar to assign the entry to a particular calendar and tap the calendar you have in mind (Home, Work, and so on). Then tap Save.**

10. **If you want to enter notes about the appointment or event, tap Notes. Type your note, and then tap Save.**

A virtual keyboard pops up so you can type in those notes.

11. **Tap Done when you have finished entering everything.**

You can choose a default Calendar by tapping Settings, tapping Mail, Contacts, Calendars, and by flicking the screen until the Calendar section appears. Tap Default Calendar and select the Calendar you want to show up regularly.

If you travel long distances for your job, you can also make events appear according to whatever time zone you selected for your calendars. In Calendar settings, tap Time Zone Support to turn it on, and then tap Time Zone. Type the time zone location on the keyboard that appears.

When Time Zone Support is turned off, events are displayed according to the time zone of your current location.

You can turn off a calendar alert by tapping Settings, tapping Sounds, and then making sure that the Calendar Alerts button is turned Off.

If you want to modify an existing calendar entry, tap the entry, tap Edit, and then make whatever changes need to be made. To wipe out a calendar entry, tap Edit and then tap Delete Event. You'll get a chance to confirm your choice by tapping either Delete Event (again) or Cancel.

Calendar entries you create on your iPhone are synchronized with the calendar you specified in the iTunes Info pane.

A pushy calendar

If you work for a company that uses Microsoft Exchange ActiveSync, calendar entries and meeting invitations from coworkers can be *pushed* to your device so they show on-screen moments after they're entered, even if they're entered on computers at work.

Setting up an account to facilitate this pushing of calendar entries to your iPhone is a breeze, although you should check with your company's tech or IT department to make sure that your employer allows it. Then follow these steps:

1. Tap Settings.

2. Tap Mail, Contacts, Calendars.

3. Tap Add Account.

4. From the Add Account list shown in Figure 6-7, Tap Microsoft Exchange.

5. Fill in the appropriate e-mail address, username, password, and description in the fields provided and tap Next.

6. Enter your server address on the next screen that appears. The rest of the fields should be filled in with the e-mail address, username, and password you just entered, as shown in Figure 6-8. Tap Next.

7. Tap the On switches for all the information types you want to synchronize using Microsoft Exchange, from among Mail, Contacts, and Calendars.

8. You should be good to go from here, although some employers may require you to add additional passcodes to safeguard company secrets.

Figure 6-7: The Add Accounts screen.

 If your business-issued iPhone is ever lost or stolen — or it turns out you're a double-agent working for a rival company — your employer's IT administrators can remotely wipe your device clean.

 If your company uses Microsoft Exchange 2007, you won't have to enter the address of your Exchange server. iPhone can determine it automatically.

 Only one account taking advantage of Microsoft Exchange ActiveSync can be configured to work on your iPhone.

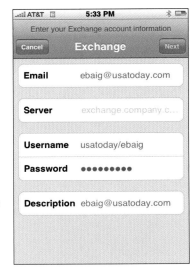

Figure 6-8: Fill in the blanks to set up your corporate account.

Responding to meeting invitations

There's one more important button, located just to the right of the List, Day, and Month buttons — but you see it only when Exchange calendar syncing is turned on. The Invitations button shows up if you have an invitation on your calendar. It's represented by an arrow pointing downward into a half-rectangle.

Tap the Invitation button now to view your pending invitations, and then tap any of the items on the list to get more details.

Suppose that a meeting invitation arrives from your boss. You can see who else is attending the shindig, check scheduling conflicts, and more. Tap Accept to let the meeting organizer know you're in, tap Decline if you've got something better to do (and aren't worried about upsetting the person who signs your paycheck), or tap Maybe if you're waiting for a better offer.

You can choose to receive an alert every time someone sends you an invitation. In Calendar settings, tap New Invitation Alerts so that the On button in blue is showing.

If you take advantage of Apple's $99-a-year MobileMe service (formerly .Mac), you can keep calendar entries synchronized between your iPhone and PC or Mac. So when you make a scheduling change on your iPhone, it's automatically updated on your computer, and vice versa. Choose MobileMe from the Add Account screen listed earlier in Step 4 to get started.

You learn more about configuring MobileMe when we discuss the Fetch New Data setting in Chapter 13.

Apple was grappling with some MobileMe snags as this book was being published. We're confident they'll have been resolved by the time you read this.

Calculate This

Quick, what's 3,467.8 times 982.3? Why, the answer (of course) is 3,406,419.94.

We can solve the problem quickly thanks to the iPhone's calculator, buried (until needed) under another of those Home screen icons.

Your handy iPhone calculator does just fine for adding, subtracting, multiplying, and dividing. Numbers and symbols (such as a C for clear, and M+ for memory) are large and easy to see.

But you might be thinking: "This isn't exactly the most advanced calculator I've ever used." And you'd be right. It can't handle a sine or a square root, much less more advanced functions.

Fortunately the math whizzes at Apple were thinking right along with you. To see what they came up with, rotate the iPhone. As if by sleight of hand, your pocket calculator is now a full-fledged scientific calculator capable of tackling dozens of complex functions. Take a gander at both calculators in Figure 6-9.

Figure 6-9: Solving simple — and more complex — mathematical problems.

Isn't it nice to know just how much smarter a smartphone can make you feel?

Punching the Clock

Here's another thing you must be thinking: "So the iPhone has a clock. Big whoop. Doesn't every cell phone have a clock?"

Well, yes, every cell phone does have a clock. But not every phone has a *world clock* that lets you display the time in multiple cities on multiple continents. And not every cell phone has an alarm, a stopwatch, and a timer to boot.

Let's take a look at the time functions on your iPhone.

World clock

Want to know the time in Beijing or Bogota? Tapping on World Clock (inside the Clock application) lets you display the time in numerous cities around the globe, as shown in Figure 6-10.

Tap the + symbol at the upper-right corner of the screen and start typing a city name with the virtual keyboard. The moment you type the first letter, in fact, the iPhone displays a list of cities or countries that begin with that letter. So typing *V* will bring up both Vancouver, Canada, and Caracas, Venezuela, among myriad other possibilities. You can create clocks for as many cities as you like, though the times in only four cities appear in a single screen. To see times in other cities, scroll up or down.

To remove a city from the list, tap Edit, and then tap the red circle with the white horizontal line in it to the left of the city you want to drop. Then tap Delete.

Figure 6-10: What time is it in Budapest?

You can also rearrange the order of the cities displaying the time. Tap Edit, and then press your finger against the symbol with three horizontal lines to the right of the city you want to move up or down in the list. Then drag the city to its new spot.

Alarm clock

Ever try to set the alarm in a hotel room? It's remarkable how complicated setting an alarm can be, on even the most inexpensive clock radio. As with most things, the procedure is dirt simple on the iPhone:

1. **Tap Clock on the Home screen to display the Clock application.**

2. **Tap the Alarm icon at the bottom of the screen.**

3. **Tap the + sign at the upper-right corner of the screen.**

4. **Choose the time of the alarm by rotating the wheel on the bottom half of the screen.**

   This is similar to the action required to setting the time an event starts or ends in your calendar.

5. **If you want the alarm to go off on other days, tap Repeat and tell the iPhone the days you want the alarm to be repeated.**

6. **Tap Sound to choose the ringtone (see Chapter 4) that will wake you up. You can even use the custom ringtone you created yourself.**

   This is a matter of personal preference, but we can tell you that the ringtone with the appropriate name Alarm managed to wake Ed out of a deep sleep.

7. **Tap Snooze to have the alarm appear on the screen accompanied by a Snooze button.**

   Tap the Snooze button to shut up the alarm for 9 minutes.

8. **If you want to call the alarm something other than, um, Alarm, tap the Label field and use the virtual keyboard to type another descriptor.**

9. **Tap Save when the alarm settings are to your liking.**

You'll know that an alarm has been set and activated thanks to the tiny status icon — surprise, surprise, it looks like a clock — that appears in the upper-right corner of the screen.

An alarm takes precedence over any tracks you are listening to on the iPod. So songs momentarily pause when an alarm goes off and resume when you turn off the alarm (or press the Snooze button).

When your Ring/Silent switch is set to silent, your iPhone doesn't ring, play alert effects, or make iPod sounds. But it *will* play alarms from the Clock application. That's good to know when you set your phone to Silent at a movie or the opera. And although it seems obvious, if you want to actually *hear* an alarm, you have to make sure your iPhone's volume is turned up.

Stopwatch

If you're helping a loved one train for a marathon, your iPhone's Stopwatch function can provide an assist. It's accessible by tapping Stopwatch in the Clock application.

Just tap Start to begin the count and tap Stop at the finish line. You can also tap a Lap button to monitor the times between laps.

Timer

Cooking a hard-boiled egg or Thanksgiving turkey? Again, the iPhone comes to the rescue. Tap Timer (within the Clock app) and then rotate the hour and minute wheels until the time you have in mind is highlighted. Tap When Timer Ends to choose the ringtone that will signify that time's up.

After you've set up the length of the timer, tap Start when you're ready to begin. You can watch the minutes and seconds wind down on the screen if you have nothing better to do.

But if you're doing anything else on the iPhone — admiring photos, say — you hear the ringtone and see a *Timer Done* message on the screen at the appropriate moment. Tap OK to silence the ringtone.

Now it's time to move on to the stuff that makes the iPhone really sexy — and fun: songs, video, and photos.

Part III
The Multimedia iPhone

The 5th Wave   By Rich Tennant

"Okay, the view's just up ahead. Everyone switch to 'America the Beautiful' on your iPhone playlist."

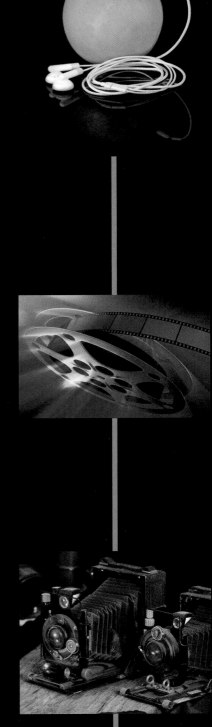

Your iPhone is arguably the best iPod ever invented. So in this part we look at the multimedia side of your phone — audio, video, and still pictures, too. There has never been a phone that was this much fun to use; in this part we show you how to wring the most out of every multimedia bit of it.

First we explore how to enjoy listening to music, podcasts, and audiobooks on your iPhone. Then we look at some video, both literally and figuratively. We start off with a quick segment about how to find good video for your iPhone, followed by instructions for watching video on your iPhone.

Before we leave the video scene, you also see how to have a blast with video from the famous YouTube Web site, using iPhone's built-in YouTube application. We wrap up this multimedia part with everything you always wanted to know about photos and iPhones: how to shoot them well, how to store them, how to sync them, and how to do all kinds of other interesting things with them.

Get in Tune(s): Audio on Your iPhone

As we mention elsewhere, your iPhone is also one heck of an iPod — especially when it comes to audio and video. In this chapter, we show you how to use your iPhone for audio; in Chapter 8 we cover video.

We start with a quick tour of the iPhone's iPod application. Then we look at how to use your iPhone as an audio player. After you're nice and comfy with using it this way, we show you how to customize the listening experience so it's just the way you like it. Finally, we offer a few tips to help you get the most out of using your iPhone as an audio player.

We're going to assume that you've synced your iPhone with your computer and that your iPhone contains audio content — songs, podcasts, or audiobooks. If you don't have any audio on your iPhone yet, we humbly suggest that you get some (flip back to Chapter 3 and follow the instructions) before you read the rest of this chapter — or the next chapter, for that matter.

Okay, now that you have some audio content on your iPhone to play with, are you ready to rock?

©Stockphoto.com/HannahmariaH

Introducing the iPod inside Your iPhone

To use your iPhone as an iPod, just tap the iPod icon in the bottom-right corner of the Home screen. At the bottom of the screen that appears, you should see five icons: Playlists, Artists, Songs, Video, and More.

If you don't see these icons, tap the Back button in the top-left corner of the screen (the one that looks like a little arrow pointing to the left).

Or, if you're holding your iPhone sideways (the long edges parallel to the ground), rotate it 90 degrees so it's upright (the short edges parallel to the ground).

You'll understand why your iPhone's orientation matters when you read the section on Cover Flow, which is coming up in a few pages.

Playing with playlists

Tap the Playlists icon at the bottom of the screen and a list of playlists appears. If you don't have any playlists on your iPhone, don't sweat it. Just know that if you had some, this is where they'd be. (Playlists let you organize songs around a particular theme or mood: opera arias, romantic ballads, British Invasion, whatever. Younger folks call 'em *mixes*.)

Tap a playlist and you see a list of the songs it contains. If the list is longer than one screen, flick upwards to scroll down. Tap a song in the list and it plays.

And that's all there is to selecting and playing a song from a playlist.

Artistic license

Now let's find and play a song by the artist's name instead of by playlist. Tap the Artists icon at the bottom of the screen and a list of artists appears.

Tap an artist's name and a list of songs by that artist appears. If the list is longer than one screen, flick upwards to scroll down. Tap a song in this list and it plays.

Are you starting to see a pattern here?

Song selection

Finally, let's find a song by its title and play it. Tap the Songs icon at the bottom of the screen and a list of songs appears.

Now, chances are your list of songs is quite a bit longer than your lists of playlists and artists. So in addition to flicking upwards to scroll down, you can tap a letter on the right side of the screen to jump to songs that start with that letter. In Figure 7-1, for example, that letter is *M*.

Notice that those letters are extremely small, so unless you have very tiny fingers you may have to settle for a letter close to the one you want or tap several times before you get it added.

Tap

Figure 7-1: Tap the *M* on the right side of the screen to jump to song titles that begin with *M*.

Taking Control of Your Tunes

Now that you have the basics down, here's a look at some of the other things you can do when your iPhone is in its iPod mode.

Go with the (cover) flow

Finding tracks by playlist, artist, or song is cool, but finding them with Cover Flow is even cooler. Cover Flow lets you browse your music collection by its album artwork. To use Cover Flow, turn your iPhone sideways (that is, long edges parallel to the ground). As long as you're not browsing or viewing video (and, of course, you've tapped the iPod icon on the Home screen so your iPhone behaves like an iPod), Cover Flow fills the screen, as shown in Figure 7-2.

Play/Pause   Info

Figure 7-2: Go with the Cover Flow.

It's simple to flip through your cover art in Cover Flow. All you have to do is drag or flick your finger left or right on the screen and the covers go flying by. Flick or drag quickly and the covers whiz by; flick or drag slowly and the covers move leisurely. Or tap a particular cover on the left or right of the current (centered) cover and that cover jumps to the center.

Try it, you'll like it! Now here's how to put Cover Flow to work for you:

- ✔ To see the tracks (songs) on an album, tap the cover when it's centered or tap the info button (the little *i*) in the lower-right corner of the screen. The track list appears.

- ✔ To play a track, tap its name in the list. If the list is long, scroll by dragging or flicking up and down on it.

- ✔ To go back to Cover Flow, tap the title bar at the top of the track list or tap the little *i* button again.

- ✔ To play or pause the current song, tap the Play/Pause button in the lower-left corner.

If no cover art exists for an album in your collection, the iPhone displays a plain-looking cover decorated with a single musical note. The name of the album appears below this generic cover.

And that, friends, is all there is to the iPhone's cool Cover Flow mode.

Flow's not here right now

As you saw earlier in the chapter, when you hold your iPhone vertically (the short edges parallel to the ground) and tap the Playlists, Artists, or Songs button, you see a list instead of Cover Flow.

The controls are different depending on which way you hold your iPhone as well. When you hold your iPhone vertically, as shown in Figure 7-3, you see controls that don't appear when you hold your iPhone sideways. Furthermore, the controls you see when viewing the Playlists, Artists, or Songs lists are slightly different from the controls you see when a song is playing.

Here's how to use the controls that appear when the iPhone is vertical:

- ✔ **Back button:** Tap this to return to whichever list you used last — Playlists, Artists, or Songs.

- ✔ **Switch to Track List button:** Tap this to switch to a list of tracks.

    If you don't see the next three controls — the Repeat button, the Scrubber, and the Shuffle button — tap the album cover once to make them appear.

✏ **Repeat button:** Tap once to repeat songs in the current album or list. The button turns blue. Tap it again to repeat the current song over and over again; the blue button displays the number 1 when it's in this mode. Tap it again to turn it off. The button goes back to its original color, gray.

✏ **Scrubber bar:** Drag the little dot (the playhead) along the Scrubber bar to skip to any point within the song.

✏ **Shuffle button:** Tap once to shuffle songs and play them in random order. The button turns blue when shuffling is enabled. Tap it again to play songs in order again. The button goes back to its original color, gray.

You can also shuffle tracks in any list of songs — such as playlists or albums — by tapping the word *Shuffle,* which appears at the top of the list. Regardless of whether the Shuffle button has been tapped, this technique always plays songs in that list in random order.

Figure 7-3: Hold your iPhone vertically when you play a track and you see these controls.

✏ **Restart/Previous Track/Rewind button:** Tap this once to go to the beginning of the track. Tap it twice to go to the start of the previous track in the list. Touch and hold it to rewind through the song at double speed.

✏ **Play/Pause button:** Tap this to play or pause the song.

✏ **Next Track/Fast Forward button:** Tap this to skip to the next track in the list. Touch and hold it to fast-forward through the song at double speed.

✏ **Volume control:** Drag the little dot left or right to reduce or increase the volume level.

If you're using the headset included with your iPhone, you can squeeze the mic to pause, and squeeze it again to play. You can also squeeze it twice in rapid succession to skip to the next song. Sweet!

When you tap the Switch to Track List button, the iPhone screen and the controls change, as shown in Figure 7-4. And here's how to use *those* controls:

Figure 7-4: Tap the Switch to Track List button and these new controls appear.

- **Switch to Now Playing button:** Tap this to switch to the Now Playing screen for the current track (refer to Figure 7-3).

- **Rating bar:** Drag across the rating bar to rate the current track with zero to five stars. The track shown in Figure 7-4 has a four-star rating.

The tracks are the songs in the current list (album, playlist, artist, and so on) and the current track indicator shows you which song is currently playing (or paused). Tap any song in a track list to play it.

And that, gentle reader, is pretty much all you need to know to enjoy listening to music (and podcasts and audiobooks, too) on your iPhone.

Customizing Your Audio Experience

We should cover a few more things before you move on to the video side of your iPhone-as-an-iPod in Chapter 8. In this section you find a bunch of stuff you can do to make your listening experience even better.

If you still want more . . .

If you'd prefer to browse through your audio collection by criteria other than playlists, artists, or songs, there is a way. That way is to tap the More button at the bottom-right corner of the screen. The More list appears. Tap a choice in the list — albums, audiobooks, compilations, composers, genres, or podcasts — and your audio collection is organized by your criterion.

But wait, there's more. You can swap out the Playlists, Artists, Songs, and Video buttons for ones that better suit your needs. So, for example, if you listen to a lot of podcasts and never watch video, you can replace the Video button with a Podcasts button.

Here's how:

1. **Tap the More button at the bottom-right corner of the screen.**
2. **Tap the Edit button at the top-left corner of the screen.**
3. **Drag any button on the screen — Albums, Podcasts, Audiobooks, Genres, Composers, Compilations — onto the button at the bottom of the screen that you want it to replace.**
4. **You can also rearrange the five buttons now by dragging them to the left or right.**
5. **When you have everything just the way you like it, tap the Done button to return to the More list.**

You can always browse your audio collection by buttons you replace this way by tapping the More button and choosing the item that corresponds to the button you replaced in the More list.

Setting preferences

You can change a few preference settings to customize your iPhone-as-an-iPod experience.

Play all songs at the same volume level

iTunes has an option called Sound Check that automatically adjusts the level of songs so they play at the same volume relative to each other. That way, one song never blasts out your ears even if the recording level is much louder than that of the song before or after it. To tell the iPhone to use these volume settings, you first have to turn on the feature in iTunes on your computer. Here's how to do that:

1. **Choose iTunes⇨Preferences (Mac) or Edit⇨Preferences (PC).**
2. **Click the Playback tab.**
3. **Select the Sound Check check box to enable it.**

Now you need to tell the iPhone to use the Sound Check settings from iTunes. Here's how to do *that*:

1. **Tap the Settings icon on the iPhone's Home screen.**
2. **Tap iPod in the list of settings.**
3. **Tap Sound Check to turn it on.**

Set the audiobook playing speed

You can make audiobooks play a bit faster or slower than usual if you like. To do so:

1. **Tap the Settings icon on the Home screen.**

2. **Tap iPod in the list of settings.**

3. **Tap Audiobook in the list of iPod settings.**

4. **Tap Slower or Faster to slow down or speed up audiobook playback.**

Choose an equalizer setting

An equalizer increases or decreases the relative levels of specific frequencies to enhance the sound you hear. Some equalizer settings emphasize the bass notes (low end) in a song; other equalizer settings make the higher frequencies more apparent. The iPhone has more than a dozen equalizer presets, with names such as Acoustic, Bass Booster, Bass Reducer, Dance, Electronic, Pop, and Rock. Each one is ostensibly tailored to a specific type of music.

The way to find out whether you prefer using equalization is to listen to music while trying out different settings. To do that, first start listening to a song you like. Then, while the song is playing, follow these steps:

1. **Tap the Home button on the front of your iPhone.**

2. **Tap the Settings icon on the Home screen.**

3. **Tap iPod in the list of settings.**

4. **Tap EQ in the list of iPod settings.**

5. **Tap different EQ presets (Pop, Rock, R&B, Dance, and so on) and listen carefully to the way it changes how the song sounds.**

6. **When you find an equalizer preset you think sounds good, tap the Home button and you're finished.**

If you don't like any of the presets, tap Off at the top of the EQ list to turn off the equalizer.

If you've set an equalizer preset for a song using the Track Info window in iTunes, that setting is applied automatically to the song when you sync it to your iPhone. That's pretty cool. Alas, *custom* equalizer settings — ones you create in iTunes that are not presets like Rock, Pop, Bass Booster, and such — *won't* be applied on the iPhone.

Set a volume limit for music (and videos)

You can instruct your iPhone to limit the loudest listening level for audio or video. To do so, here's the drill:

1. **Tap the Settings icon on the Home screen.**

2. **Tap iPod in the list of settings.**

3. **Tap Volume Limit in the list of iPod settings.**

4. **Drag the slider to adjust the maximum volume level to your liking.**

5. **(Optional) Tap Lock Volume Limit to assign a four-digit passcode to this setting so others can't easily change it.**

The Volume Limit setting only limits the volume of music and videos. It doesn't apply to podcasts or audiobooks. And although it does work with any headset, headphones, or speakers plugged into the headset jack on your iPhone, it does not affect sound played through your iPhone's internal speaker.

Make a playlist on your iPhone

Of course you can make playlists in iTunes and sync them with your iPhone, but you can also create playlists on your iPhone when you're out and about. Here's how:

1. **Tap the iPod icon in the bottom-right corner of the Home screen.**

2. **Tap the Playlists button at the bottom of the screen.**

3. **Tap the first item in the list, On-the-Go.**

   An alphabetical list of all the songs on your iPhone appears. To the right of each song is a little plus sign.

4. **Tap the plus sign next to a song name to add the song to your On-the-Go playlist.**

   To add all of these songs to your On-the-Go playlist, tap the plus sign next to the first item in the list, Add All Songs.

5. **Tap the Done button in the top-right corner.**

If you create an On-the-Go playlist and then sync your iPhone with your computer, that playlist is saved both on the iPhone and in iTunes on your computer. The first time you save one, it is named On-the-Go 1 automatically. Subsequent lists you create are auto-named On-the-Go 2, On-the-Go 3, and so on.

The playlists remain until you delete them from iTunes. To do that, select the playlist's name in the source list and then press Delete or Backspace.

You can also edit your On-the-Go playlist. To do so, first tap the Playlists button at the bottom of the screen, tap the first item in the list, On-the-Go, and tap the Edit button. Then:

- ✓ **To move a song up or down in the On-the-Go playlist:** A little icon with three gray bars appears to the right of each song. Drag the icon up to move the song higher in the list or down to move the song lower in the list.

- ✓ **To add more songs to the On-the-Go playlist:** Tap the plus button in the top-left corner.

- ✓ **To delete a song from the On-the-Go playlist:** Tap the minus sign to the left of the song name. Note that deleting a song from the On-the-Go playlist doesn't remove the song from your iPhone.

- ✓ **To clear the On-the-Go playlist of all songs:** Tap the first item in the list, Clear Playlist.

When you've finished editing, tap the Done button in the top-right corner.

And that's all you have to do to create and manage On-the-Go playlists.

Set a sleep timer

If you like to fall asleep with music playing but don't want to leave your iPhone playing music all night long, you can turn on its sleep timer.

Here's how:

1. **Tap the Clock button on the Home screen.**
2. **Tap the Timer icon in the lower-right corner.**
3. **Set the number of hours and minutes you want the iPhone-as-an-iPod to play, and then tap the When Timer Ends button.**
4. **Tap the first item in the list, Sleep iPod.**
5. **Tap the Set button in the top-right corner.**
6. **Tap the big green Start button.**

That's it! After the appropriate period of time, your iPod stops playing and your iPhone goes to sleep.

iPhone Video: Seeing Is Believing

*P*icture this scene: The smell of popcorn permeates the room as you and your family congregate to watch the latest Hollywood blockbuster. A motion picture soundtrack swells up. The images on the screen are stunning. And all eyes are fixed on the iPhone.

Okay, here comes the reality check. The iPhone is not going to replace a wall-sized high-definition television as the centerpiece of your home theater. But we do want to emphasize that with its glorious widescreen $3^1/_2$-inch display — the best we've seen on a handheld device — watching movies and other videos on the iPhone can be a cinematic delight.

Let's get on with the show!

Finding Stuff to Watch

The video you'll watch on the iPhone generally falls into one of four categories:

  ✔ **Movies, TV shows, and music videos that reside in iTunes software on your PC or Mac that you synchronize with your iPhone.** (For more on synchronization, refer to Chapter 3.) You can watch these by tapping the iPod icon at the bottom of the Home screen and then tapping Videos.

©iStockphoto.com/phi2

Are we compatible?

Sidebars in this book are considered optional reading, but we secretly hope you'll digest every word because you may discover something, or be entertained, or both. But you can safely skip the material contained herein — no matter how much you want to curry favor with your teachers, um, authors.

Still, we present this list of video formats supported by the iPhone as a courtesy to those with geek aspirations (you know who you are). And just to point out how absurd the world of tech can sound sometimes — even from a consumer-friendly company such as Apple — we are quoting this passage from Apple's Web site verbatim:

Video formats supported: H.264 video, up to 1.5 Mbps, 640 by 480 pixels, 30 frames per second, Low-Complexity version of the H.264 Baseline Profile with AAC-LC audio up to 160 Kbps, 48kHz, stereo audio in .m4v, .mp4, and .mov file formats; H.264 video, up to 2.5 Mbps, 640 by 480 pixels, 30 frames per second, Baseline Profile up to Level 3.0 with AAC-LC audio up to 160 Kbps, 48kHz, stereo audio in .m4v, .mp4, and .mov file

formats; MPEG-4 video, up to 2.5 Mbps, 640 by 480 pixels, 30 frames per second, Simple Profile with AAC-LC audio up to 160 Kbps, 48kHz, stereo audio in .m4v, .mp4, and .mov file formats.

Got all that? Here's the takeaway message: The iPhone works with a whole bunch of video, although not everything you'll want to watch will make it through. And you may not know if it will play until you try. Indeed, several Internet video standards — notably Adobe Flash, Java, Real, and Windows Media Video — were not supported when this book was in production. And we should probably point out that some video that will play on an iPod Classic or iPod nano might not play in the iPhone for technical reasons we won't bore you with right now. (This may have changed by the time you read this.)

Then again, with the appropriate utility software, you may be able to convert some non-working video to an iPhone-friendly format. If something doesn't play now, it may well in the future — because Apple has the capability to upgrade the iPhone through software.

Apple's own iTunes Store features dedicated sections for purchasing episodes of TV shows (from *The Larry Sanders Show* to *Dora the Explorer*) and movies (such as *Atonement* or *Ratatouille*). Typical price as of this writing is $1.99 per episode for TV shows and $9.99 to $14.99 for feature films.

You can also rent some movies, typically for $2.99 or $3.99. You'll have 30 days to begin watching a rented flick, and 24 hours to finish once you've started. Such films appear in their own Rented Movies section on the video list, which you get to by tapping iTunes and then Videos. The number of days before your rental expires is displayed.

✔ **The boatload of video podcasts, just about all of them free, featured in the iTunes Store.** Podcasts started out as another form of Internet radio, although instead of listening to live streams, you downloaded files onto your computer or iPod to take in at your leisure. There are still lots of audio podcasts, but the focus here is on video.

✔ **Homegrown videos from the popular YouTube Internet site.** Apple obviously thinks highly of YouTube because it devoted a dedicated Home screen icon to the site. More on YouTube's special place in the iPhone later in this chapter.

✔ **The movies you've created in iMovie software or other software on the Mac or, for that matter, other programs on the PC.** Plus all the other videos you may have downloaded from the Internet.

You may have to prepare these videos so that they'll play on your iPhone. To do so, highlight the video in question after it resides in your iTunes library. Go to the Advanced menu in iTunes, and click Convert Selection for iPod/iPhone.

For more on compatibility, check out the "Are we compatible?" sidebar in this chapter (but read it at your own risk).

Playing Video

Now that you know what you want to watch, here's how to watch it:

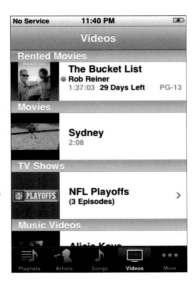

Figure 8-1: Choosing the video to watch.

1. **On the Home screen, tap the iPod icon and then tap the Videos icon.**

   Your list of videos pops up. As shown in Figure 8-1, videos are segregated by category (Movies, TV Shows, Music Videos, Podcasts) and accompanied by thumbnail images and the length of the video.

2. **Flick your finger to scroll through the list, and then tap the video you want to play.**

   You'll see a spinning circle for just a moment and then the video will begin.

3. **Turn the device to its side because the iPhone plays video only in landscape, or widescreen, mode.**

   For movies, this is a great thing. You can watch flicks as the filmmaker intended, in a cinematic *aspect ratio*.

4. Now that the video is playing, tap the screen to display the controls shown in Figure 8-2.

5. Tap the controls that follow as needed:

- To play or pause the video, tap the Play/Pause button.

- Drag the volume slider to the right to raise the volume and to the left to lower it. Alternatively, use the physical Volume buttons to control the audio levels. If the video is oriented properly, the buttons will be to the bottom left of the iPhone.

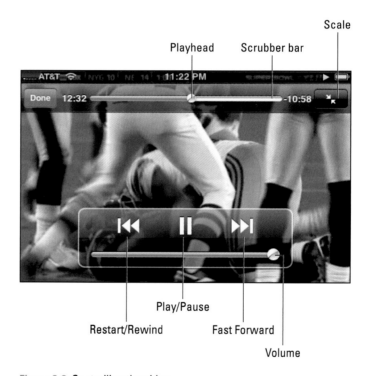

Figure 8-2: Controlling the video.

- Tap the Restart/Rewind button to restart the video or tap and hold the same button to rewind.

- Tap and hold the Fast Forward button to advance the video. You can skip ahead also by dragging the playhead along the Scrubber bar.

- Tap the Scale button to toggle between filling the entire screen with video or fitting the video to the screen. Alternatively, you can double-tap the video to go back and forth between fitting and filling the screen.

Here's the distinction between fitting and filling. Fitting the video to the screen displays the film in its theatrical aspect ratio. But you may see black bars above or below the video (or to its sides), which some people don't like. On the other hand, filling the entire screen with the video may crop or trim the sides or top of the picture, so you aren't seeing the complete scene that the director shot.

6. **Tap the screen again to make the controls go away (or just wait for them to go away on their own).**

7. **Tap Done when you've finished watching (you'll have to summon the controls back if they're not already present).**

    You return to the iPhone's video menu screen.

To delete a video manually, swipe left or right over the video listing. Then tap the small red Delete button that materializes. To confirm your intention, tap the larger Delete button that appears.

Sometimes you want to hear a song from a music video but don't want to watch it. Instead of tapping the Videos icon to grab that selection, choose the ditty by tapping the Songs or Artists icon instead.

Hey You, It's YouTube

YouTube has come to define video sharing on the Internet. The wildly popular site, now owned by Google, has become so powerful that American presidential hopefuls and even politicians in other countries campaign and hold debates there. As you might imagine, YouTube has also generated controversy. The site has been banned in some foreign countries. And Viacom sued YouTube for more than $1 billion over alleged copyright infringements. (We'll leave that fight to the lawyers.)

All the while, of course, YouTube staked a humongous claim on mainstream culture. That's because YouTube is, well, about you and us and our pets and so on. It is the cyberdestination, as YouTube boldly proclaims, to "Broadcast Yourself."

Apple has afforded YouTube its own cherished icon on the Home screen. Somewhere north of 50 million videos are available on the iPhone, pretty much the complete YouTube catalog.

The back catalog of YouTube videos was converted to the *H.264* video-compression standard that the iPhone, the iPod Touch (and another Apple product called Apple TV) can recognize.

As with other videos, you can tap the screen when a YouTube video plays to bring up hidden video controls. Many of these controls are identical to the controls in Figure 8-2. But as Figure 8-3 shows, YouTube displays special controls of its own, notably for adding bookmarks and sending e-mail links of the video you're watching.

Bookmark   E-mail

Figure 8-3: YouTube video controls.

Hunting for YouTube gems

So where exactly do YouTubers find the videos that will offer them a blissful, albeit brief, respite from the rest of their day? By tapping on any of the following:

- **Featured:** Videos recommended by YouTube's own staffers.

- **Most Viewed:** What the YouTube community is watching. Tap All to see the most watched YouTube videos of all time. Tap Today or This Week to check out the videos most currently in vogue.

- **Bookmarks:** After stumbling on a video you like, bookmark it by tapping the Bookmark control.

- **Search:** Tap the Search icon, and then tap the blank YouTube search field at the top of the screen. Up pops one of the iPhone's virtual keyboards. Type a search phrase and then tap the Search button to generate results. (In Figure 8-4, we typed *Steve Jobs*.)

✔ **More:** Tapping More leads to more buttons or icons. As in those that follow. . . .

✔ **Most Recent:** Newly submitted videos.

✔ **Top Rated:** The people's choice. YouTube's audience chooses the best.

✔ **History:** Videos you recently viewed.

Figure 8-4: Finding Steve Jobs on YouTube.

Only four YouTube icons (besides the More button) appear at the bottom of the screen at any one time. If you'd prefer a different button than one of the four shown — Top Rated instead of Bookmarks, say — you can make it one of your Fab Four icons.

To change the icons shown on that first YouTube screen, tap More and then tap Edit. Then simply drag your preferred icon (Top Rated in this example) over the one you want to relegate to the YouTube bench (Bookmarks in this case). You can also rearrange the order of the icons by dragging them left or right.

While the movie you've selected is downloading — and how fast it arrives depends on your network coverage from AT&T or Wi-Fi, as discussed in greater detail in Chapter 10 — you see a black-and-gray screen with video controls and the YouTube logo. This screen is shown in Figure 8-5. The controls disappear when the movie starts playing.

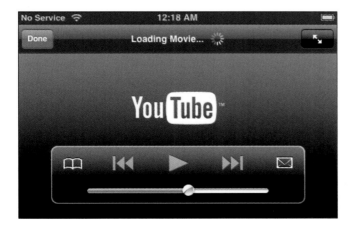

Figure 8-5: Waiting to be entertained.

Sharing YouTube videos

We were as enthralled as that harshest of critics Simon Cowell was by Paul Potts, the British mobile-phone worker turned opera singer. His star turn on the *American Idol*-like *Britain's Got Talent* has been immortalized on YouTube by millions.

You can share such a video as you are watching it, by tapping the E-mail button (refer to Figure 8-3). When you do so, one of the iPhone's virtual keyboards pops up. iPhone has already filled in the e-mail subject line with the name of the video. And the body of the message is populated with a link to the video on YouTube. All you need to do is fill in the To field with the e-mail address of the person you are sending the link to along with any additional comments.

Alternatively, from the list of videos, tap the blue button with the right-pointing arrow to see all sorts of details on a particular video. You'll see a description of the video, the number of people who viewed it, the date it was added, and other information. From there, tap the Share button to bring up the e-mail program described in the preceding paragraph.

Restricting YouTube usage

If you've given an iPhone to your kid or someone who works for you, you may not want that person spending time watching YouTube videos. You want him or her to do something more productive like homework or the quarterly budget.

That's where new parental (or might we say "Mean Boss") restrictions come in. Please note that the use of this iron-fist tool can make you really unpopular.

Tap Settings, tap General, and tap Restrictions. Then tap Enable Restrictions. You'll be asked to establish or enter a previously established passcode. Twice. Having done so, tap YouTube so that the Off button rather than the On button is what's showing. (You'll notice you can also prevent access to explicit content, the Safari browser, iTunes, and the App Store.)

Now, when you return to the Home screen, the YouTube icon is missing in action. Same goes for any other restricted activities. To restore YouTube or other privileges, go back into Restrictions, and tap Disable Restrictions. You'll have to re-enter your passcode.

These restrictions can also be applied to iTunes, Safari, and more as you see when we further delve into Settings (see Chapter 13).

With that, let's roll the closing credits to this chapter.

9

You Oughta Be in Pictures

Camera phones may outsell dedicated digital cameras nowadays, but with relatively few exceptions, they're rather mediocre picture takers. Come to think of it, most mobile phones don't show off digital images all that well either.

Of course, most mobile phones aren't iPhones.

The device you have recently purchased (or are lusting after) is a pretty spectacular photo viewer. And though its built-in digital camera isn't the one we'd rely on for snapping pictures during an African safari, say, or even Junior's fast-paced soccer game, the iPhone in your steady hands can produce perfectly acceptable photos.

©iStockphoto.com/Vasko Miokovic

Over the next few pages, you discover how best to exploit the iPhone's camera. We then move on to the real magic — making the digital photos that reside on the iPhone come alive — whether you imported them from your computer or captured them with the iPhone's camera.

Taking Your Best Shot

Like many applications on the iPhone, you'll find the Camera application icon on the Home screen. Unless you've moved things around, it's positioned on the upper row of icons all the way to the right and adjacent to its next-of-kin, the Photos icon. We'll be tapping both icons throughout this chapter.

Might as well snap an image now:

1. **Tap the Camera icon on the Home screen.**

   This tap turns the iPhone into the rough equivalent of a Kodak Instamatic, minus the film and flash, of course.

2. **Keep your eyes fixed on the iPhone's display.**

   The first thing you'll notice on the screen is something resembling a closed camera shutter. But that shutter opens in about a second, revealing a window into what the camera lens sees. In case you were wondering, the lens is hiding behind the small foxhole at the top-left corner of the back of the iPhone. (The position of the camera lens is shown in Chapter 1, Figure 1-3.)

3. **Aim the camera at whatever you want to shoot, using the iPhone's brilliant 3½-inch display as your viewfinder.**

   We've been marveling at the display throughout this book; the camera application gives us another reason to do so.

4. **When you're satisfied with what's in the frame, tap the camera icon at the bottom of the screen (see Figure 9-1) to snap the picture.**

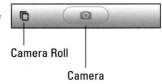

Camera Roll

Camera

    Be careful. The Camera icon is directly above the Home button. We've seen more than one iPhone user erroneously hit the Home button instead.

Figure 9-1: Say "Cheese."

   You'll experience momentary shutter lag, so be sure to remain still. When the shutter reopens, you see the image you have just shot, but just for a blink. The screen again functions as a viewfinder so that you can capture your next image.

   And that's it; you've snapped your very first iPhone picture.

5. **Repeat Steps 3 and 4 to capture additional images.**

 If you position the iPhone sideways while snapping an image, the picture is saved in landscape mode.

Tasty pixels and other digital camera treats

The iPhone is a 2-megapixel digital camera. And if you've been shopping for a digital camera of any type, you are already aware that megapixels are marketed like chocolate chips: You know, the more of them, the tastier the cookie, or (in the case of digital photography) the better the camera. But that may not always be true. The number of megapixels counts, for sure, but so do a bevy of other factors — including lens quality and shutter lag.

The important thing to remember about megapixels is that they are a measure of a camera's *resolution,* or picture sharpness, which becomes particularly important to folks who want to blow up prints well beyond snapshot size. For example, you'd probably want at least a 4-megapixel standalone digital camera if you hope to print decent 8-by-10-inch or larger photos.

Which brings us back to the iPhone. From a camera-phone perspective, 2 megapixels is still considered fairly decent, although you can certainly find more and more cell phones with a higher megapixel count. Still, we figure most of you will be more than satisfied with the pictures you take with the iPhone, as long as you keep your expectations in check and don't expect to produce poster-size images.

We're obliged to point out, however, that the digital camera in the iPhone lacks some features found on rival camera phones, notably a flash and the capability to shoot short video clips. (We are hoping a third-party developer may add this video functionality through the App Store discussed in Chapter 14.) And the iPhone has no advanced photo-editing features.

All that said, those other camera phones can't hold a candle to the iPhone when it comes to showing off those images, as the rest of this chapter proves. The iPhone's high-resolution 480-x-320 screen — yep, it's measured in pixels — is simply stunning.

There are a couple more things to keep in mind while snapping pictures with the iPhone.

In our experience, the iPhone camera button is super-sensitive. We have accidentally taken a few rotten snapshots because of that. So be careful; a gentle tap is all that's required to snap an image.

If you have trouble keeping the camera steady, try this trick. Instead of tapping the Camera icon at the bottom of the screen (as suggested previously in Step 4), keep your finger pressed against the icon and only *release* it when you're ready to snap an image.

Importing Pictures

You needn't use only the iPhone's digital camera to get pictures onto the device, of course, and in most cases, we suspect that you won't. Instead, you can synchronize photos from a PC or Macintosh using the Photos tab in the iTunes iPhone page, which is described in Chapter 3. (The assumption here is that you already know how to get pictures onto your computer.)

Quickie reminder: On a Mac, you can sync photos via iPhoto software version 4.03 or later and Aperture. And on a PC, you can sync with Adobe Photoshop Album 2.0 or later and Adobe Photoshop Elements 3.0 or later. Alternatively, with both computers, you can sync with any folder containing pictures.

When the iPhone is connected to your computer, click the Photos tab in the iTunes iPhone page. Then click the appropriate check boxes to specify the pictures and photos you want to synchronize. Or choose All Photos and Albums if you have enough storage on the iPhone to accommodate them.

Syncing pictures is a two-way process, so photos captured with the iPhone's digital camera can also end up in the photo library on your computer.

Mac users: Connecting the iPhone with photos in the Camera Roll usually launches iPhoto in addition to iTunes.

Where Have All My Pictures Gone?

So where exactly do your pictures hang out on the iPhone? The ones you snapped on iPhone end up in a photo album appropriately dubbed the Camera Roll. Of course, the photos you imported are readily available too (and grouped in the same albums they were on the computer). We'll show you not only where they are, but how to display them and share them with others — and how to dispose of the duds that don't measure up to your lofty photographic standards.

So get ready to literally get your fingers on the pix (without having to worry about smudging them):

1a. From the Camera application, tap the Camera Roll icon (refer to Figure 9-1).

The shutter closes for just an instant and is replaced by the screen depicted in Figure 9-2, which shows thumbnail images of the complete roll of pictures you've shot with the iPhone. This is the Camera Roll.

Figure 9-2: Your pictures at a glance.

1b. Alternatively, you can tap the Photos icon on the Home screen, and then tap Camera Roll or any other album in the list of Photo Albums.

Using the method described in Step 1a, you can access only the Camera Roll. Using the method described in Step 1b, you can access the Camera Roll and all your other photo albums.

2. Browse through the thumbnail images in the album until you find the picture you want to display.

If the thumbnail you have in mind doesn't appear on this screen, flick your finger up or down to scroll through the pictures rapidly or use a slower dragging motion to pore through the images more deliberately.

3. Tap the appropriate thumbnail.

The picture you've selected fills the entire screen.

4. Tap the screen again.

The picture controls appear, as shown in Figure 9-3. We discuss what these do later.

5. To make the controls disappear, tap the screen again, or just wait a few seconds and they'll go away on their own.

6. To transform the iPhone back into a picture-taker rather than a picture-viewer, make sure the picture controls are displayed and then tap the Camera icon at the upper right.

Note that this option is available only if you arrived at the Camera Roll from the Camera application. If you didn't, you have to back out of this application altogether and tap the Home button and then the Camera application icon to call the iPhone's digital camera back into duty.

7. To return to the thumbnails view of your Camera Roll or the thumbnails for any of your other albums, make sure the picture controls are displayed. Then tap the Camera Roll button at the upper left.

Return to the Camera Roll (or other album)

Next Picture

Start Slideshow

Previous Picture

Use image as wallpaper, e-mail it, assign to a contact, or send to MobileMe

Figure 9-3: Picture controls.

The Camera Roll button will carry the name of one of your other photo albums if you're trying to return to that collection of pictures instead.

Admiring Pictures

Photographs are meant to be seen, of course, not buried in the digital equivalent of a shoebox. And the iPhone affords you some neat ways to manipulate, view, and share your best photos.

You already know (from the preceding section) how to find a photo and view it full-screen and bring up picture controls. But you can do a lot of maneuvering of your pictures without summoning those controls. Here are some options:

- **Skipping ahead or viewing the previous picture:** Flick your finger left or right, or tap the left or right arrow control.

- **Landscape or portrait:** The iPhone's wizardry (or more specifically, the device's accelerometer sensor) is at work. When you turn the iPhone sideways, the picture automatically reorients itself from portrait to landscape mode, as the images in Figure 9-4 show. Pictures shot in landscape mode fill the screen when you rotate the iPhone. Rotate the device back to portrait mode, and the picture readjusts accordingly.

- **Zoom:** Double-tap to zoom in on an image and make it larger. Do so again to zoom out and make it smaller. Alternatively, take your thumb and index finger and pinch to zoom in, or un-pinch the photo to zoom out.

- **Pan and scroll:** This cool little feature is practically guaranteed to make you the life of the party. Once you've zoomed in on a picture, drag it around the screen with your finger. Besides impressing your friends, you can bring the part of the image you most care about front and center. That'll let you zoom in on Fido's adorable face as opposed to, say, the unflattering picture of the person holding the dog in his or her lap.

Figure 9-4: The same picture in portrait (left) and landscape (right) modes.

Launching Slideshows

Those of us who store a lot of photographs on computers are familiar with running slideshows of those images. It's a breeze to replicate the experience on the iPhone:

1. **Choose your Camera Roll or another album from the Photo Albums list.**

   To do so, tap the Photos icon from the Home screen or tap the Camera Roll button in the Camera application.

2. **If you see the Play button at the bottom of the thumbnails screen, tap it and you're finished.**

3. **If you don't see the Play button at the bottom of the thumbnails screen, tap a thumbnail to choose a photo, and then tap the Play button.**

   You may have to tap the picture a second time to bring up the Play button.

Enjoy the show.

Special slideshow effects

You can alter the length of time each slide is shown, change the transition effects between pictures, and display images in random order. Here's how.

From the Home screen, tap Settings and then scroll down and tap Photos. Then tap any of the following to make changes:

- **Play Each Slide For:** You have five choices (2 seconds, 3 seconds, 5 seconds, 10 seconds, 20 seconds). When you're finished, tap the Photos button to return to the main Settings screen for Photos.

- **Transition:** This is the effect you see when you move from one slide to the next. Again, there are five choices (cube, dissolve, ripple, wipe across, wipe down). Why not try them all to see what you like? Tap the Photos button when you're finished.

- **Repeat:** If this option is turned on, the slideshow continues to loop until you stop it. If it's turned off, the slide show for your Camera Roll or album plays just once. The Repeat control may be counterintuitive for some. If Off is showing, tap it to turn on the Repeat function. If On is showing, tap it to turn off the Repeat function.

- **Shuffle:** Turning this feature on plays slides in random order. As with the Repeat feature, tap Off to turn on shuffle or tap On to turn off random playback.

Tap the Home button to leave Settings and return to the Home screen.

Adding music to your slideshow

Ed loves backing up slideshows with Sinatra, Sarah Vaughan, or Gershwin, among numerous other artists. Bob loves using Beatles songs or stately classical music.

Adding music to a slideshow couldn't be easier. Just tap iPod and begin playing a song. Then return to the Photo application to start up a slideshow as described in the beginning of the "Launching Slideshows" section.

Deleting pictures

We told a tiny fib by intimating that photographs are meant to be seen. We should have amended that by saying that *some* pictures are meant to be seen. Others, well . . . you can't get rid of them fast enough. Fortunately, the iPhone makes it a cinch to bury the evidence:

1. **From the Camera Roll, tap the objectionable photograph.**

2. **Tap to display the picture controls, provided they're not already displayed.**

3. **Tap the trash can icon.**

4. **Tap Delete Photo (or Cancel if you change your mind).**

   The photo gets sucked into the trash can and mercifully disappears.

More (Not So) Stupid Picture Tricks

You can take advantage of the photos on the iPhone in a few more ways. In each case you tap the picture and make sure the picture controls are displayed. Then tap the icon at the bottom left (the one that looks like an arrow trying to escape from a rectangle). That displays the four choices shown in Figure 9-5. Here's what they do:

- **Use as Wallpaper:** The default background image on the iPhone when you unlock the device is a gorgeous view of Earth. Dramatic though it may be, you probably have an even better photograph to use as the iPhone's wallpaper. A picture of your spouse, your kids, or your pet, perhaps?

Figure 9-5: Look at what else I can do!

When you tap the Use as Wallpaper button, you see what the present image looks like as the iPhone's background picture. And as Figure 9-6 shows, you're given the opportunity to move the picture around and resize it, through the now familiar action of dragging or pinching against the screen with your fingers. When you're satisfied with what the wallpaper will look like, tap the Set Wallpaper button. Per usual, you also have the option to tap Cancel. (You can find out more about wallpaper in Chapter 13.)

Figure 9-6: Beautifying the iPhone with wallpaper.

✏ **Email Photo:** Some photos are so precious that you just have to share them with family members and friends. When you tap Email Photo, the picture is automatically embedded in the body of an outgoing e-mail message. Use the virtual keyboard to enter the e-mail addresses, subject line, and any additional comments you'd like to add. You know, something profound like, "Isn't this a great-looking photo?" (Check out Chapter 11 for more info on using e-mail.)

Alas, Apple isn't directly supporting picture messaging through what's called MMS (Multimedia Messaging Service) as we write this. By the time you read this, however, it's quite possible the capability will be included in some programs in the App Store.

✏ **Assign to Contact:** If you assign a picture to someone in your Contacts list, this image pops up when you receive a call from that person. To make it happen, tap Assign to Contact. Your list of contacts appears on the screen. Scroll up or down the list to find the person who matches the picture of the moment. As with the wallpaper example, you can drag and resize the picture to get it just right. Then tap Set Photo.

As you may recall from Chapter 4, you can also assign a photo to a contact by starting out in Contacts. As a refresher, start by tapping Phone and then tapping Contacts. From Contacts, choose the person, tap Edit, and then tap Add Photo. At that point, you can take a new picture with the iPhone's digital camera or select an existing portrait from one of your onboard picture albums.

To change the picture you've assigned to a person, tap his or her name in the Contacts list, tap Edit, and then tap the person's thumbnail picture, which also carries the label Edit. From there, you can take another photo with the iPhone's digital camera, select another photo from one of your albums, edit the photo you're already using (by resizing and dragging it to a new position), or delete the photo.

✔ **Send To MobileMe:** If you're a member of Apple's $99-a-year MobileMe service (formerly .Mac), you can publish a photo album in the MobileMe Gallery. Tap the Send To MobileMe control and tap the appropriate Gallery album to which you want to add the picture. Enter the title of the photo in the subject heading of the e-mail message box that appears. You also have to check an Album Setting box in the Gallery that has a strangely worded label: Adding of Photos via e-mail or iPhone.

Before leaving this photography section, we want to steer you to the iPhone App Store, which we explore in greater depth in Chapter 14. As of this writing, more than two dozen photography-related applications, many free, are available. These apps come from a variety of sources, including Pangea Software's Pangea VR (a utility for viewing interactive panoramas) and Connected Flow's Exposure (putting the popular Flickr service in your pocket.)

We also want to point out that many picture apps take advantage of the iPhone's location smarts. Pictures can be *geotagged* with the location in which they were shot. The first few times you use the iPhone's Camera application, it asks for your permission to use your current location. Similarly, third-party apps ask if it's okay to use your location. Later on, you might plot a picture's location on a map or use geotagged images to see where friends or like-minded individuals are hanging out.

You have just passed Photography 101 on the iPhone. We trust the coursework was a, forgive the pun, snap.

Part IV
The Internet iPhone

mercials for the iPhone say that it pro-
ou with the real Internet — and it does.
looks at the Internet components of
, starting with a chapter covering the
rowser ever to grace a handheld
ari. We reveal how to take advantage of
ookmarks and how to open multiple
at the same time. We show you how to
search on an iPhone. And we spend
sing EDGE, 3G, and Wi-Fi — the wire-
ks that are compatible with the device.

sit the Mail program and see how easy
p e-mail accounts and send and
honest-to-goodness e-mail messages
ments.

examine three superb Web-enabled
s. In Maps, you determine the busi-
restaurants you'd like to visit, get driv-
ns and the traffic en route, and take
of the iPhone's capability to find you. In
ou get the forecast for all the cities you
an on visiting. And in Stocks, you can
down on how well the equities in your
e performing.

Going On a Mobile Safari

"*T*he Internet in your pocket."

That's what Apple promised the iPhone would bring to the public when the product was announced in January 2007. Steve Jobs & Co. has come tantalizingly close to delivering on that pledge.

©iStockphoto.com/kim258

For years, the cell-phone industry has been offering some sort of watered-down mobile version of the Internet, but the approaches have fallen far short of what you've come to experience sitting in front of a computer.

Apple, however, has managed for the most part to replicate the real-deal Internet with the iPhone. Web pages look like Web pages on a Windows PC or Macintosh, right down to swanky graphics and pictures — and at least some of the video.

In this chapter, you find out how to navigate through cyberspace on your iPhone.

TECHNICAL STUFF

Living on the EDGE

You can't typically make or receive phone calls on a wireless phone without tapping into a cellular network. And you can't prowl the virtual corridors of cyberspace (or send e-mail) on a mobile phone without accessing a wireless *data* network. In the U.S., the iPhone works with Wi-Fi, AT&T's EDGE, and AT&T's 3G. (It also works with another wireless technology called *Bluetooth,* but that serves a different purpose and is addressed in Chapter 13.) The iPhone also works with a data network called GPRS.

The iPhone automatically hops onto the fastest available network, which is almost always Wi-Fi. *Wi-Fi* is the friendly moniker applied to the far geekier *802.11* designation. And "eight-oh-two-dot-eleven" (as it is pronounced) is followed by a letter, typically (but not always) *b, g,* or *n.* So you'll see it written as 802.11b, 802.11g, and so on. The letters relate to differing technical standards that have to do with the speed and range you can expect out of the Wi-Fi configuration. But we certainly wouldn't have you lose any sleep over this if you haven't boned up on this geeky alphabet.

For the record, the iPhone adheres to 802.11b and 802.11g standards, which means it works with most common Internet routers available to the masses and most public and private Internet *hotspots,* found at airports, colleges, coffeehouses, and elsewhere. If you have to present a password to take advantage of a for-fee hotspot, you can enter it via the iPhone's virtual keyboard.

The problem with Wi-Fi is that it is far from ubiquitous, which leads us right back to EDGE or 3G. If you're ever on a million-dollar game show and have to answer the question, EDGE is shorthand for *Enhanced Datarate for GSM Evolution.* It's based on the global *GSM* phone standard.

Meanwhile, 3G stands for third generation; 3G Web sites typically download two times faster than EDGE in our experience, and sometimes faster than that. But again, Wi-Fi downloads are even zippier.

The bottom line is this: Depending on where you live, work, or travel, you may feel like you are teetering on the EDGE in terms of acceptable Internet coverage, especially if Wi-Fi and/or true 3G are beyond your reach. We've used the iPhone in areas where Web pages load really slowly, not-so-vaguely reminiscent of dial-up telephone modems for your computer.

You may wonder why Apple and AT&T chose EDGE for the iPhone in the first place? One reason was that EDGE blanketed a good part of the country, whereas 3G's "footprint" was far smaller. And the 3G networks also hog more power than EDGE, putting a serious crimp on the iPhone's battery life. Of course, Wi-Fi can put strains on a battery too. Finally, 3G networks weren't standardized until pretty far into the iPhone's development. Even now, in our experience, Internet coverage can be a bit flaky.

Surfin' Dude

A version of Apple's Safari Web browser is a major reason the Net is the Net on the iPhone. Safari for the Mac, and (more recently) for Windows, is one of the best Web browsers in the computer business. And in our view it has no rival as a cell-phone browser.

Exploring the browser

It is worth starting our cyber-expedition with a quick tour of the Safari browser. Take a gander at Figure 10-1: Not all the browser controls found on a PC or Mac are present. Still, the iPhone's Safari has a familiar look and feel. We get to these and other controls throughout this chapter.

Before plunging in, we recommend a little detour. Read the "Living on the EDGE" sidebar to find out more about the wireless networks that let you surf the Web on the iPhone in the first place.

Blasting off into cyberspace

So, we've told you how great Web pages look on the iPhone and you're eager to get going. We won't hold you back much longer.

When you start by tapping the address field, the virtual keyboard appears. You may

Search Google or Yahoo!

Address field

Reload Web Page

Previous Web Page

Next Web Page

Bookmarks

Go to Add Bookmark Page

Pages

Navigation bar

Figure 10-1: The iPhone's Safari browser.

notice one thing about the keyboard right off the bat. Because so many Web addresses end with the suffix *.com* (pronounced "dotcom"), the virtual keyboard has a dedicated .com key. For other common Web suffixes, such as *.edu, .net,* and *.org,* press and hold the .com key and choose the relevant domain type.

Of equal importance, both the . (period) and the / (slash) are on the virtual keyboard because you frequently use them when you enter Web addresses.

The moment you tap a single letter, you see a list of Web addresses that match those letters. For example, if you tap the letter *E* (as we did in the example in Figure 10-2), you see Web listings for EarthLink, eBay, and so on. Tapping *U* or *H* instead may bring up URLs for *USA TODAY* or the *Houston Chronicle,* shameless plugs for the newspapers where Ed and Bob are columnists.

The iPhone has two ways to determine Web sites to suggest when you tap letters. One method is the Web sites you've already bookmarked from the Safari or Internet Explorer browsers on your computer (and synchronized as described in Chapter 3). More on bookmarks later in this chapter.

Figure 10-2: Web pages that match your search letter.

The second method iPhone uses when suggesting Web sites when you tap a particular letter is to suggest sites from the History list — those cyberdestinations you've recently hung your hat in. Because history repeats itself, we also tackle that topic later in the chapter.

You might as well open your first Web page now — and a full HTML page at that, to borrow from techie lingo:

1. **Tap the Safari icon at the bottom of the Home screen.**

   It's another member of the Fantastic Four (along with Phone, Mail, and iPod).

2. **Tap the address field (labeled in Figure 10-1).**

   If you can't see the address field, tap the status bar or scroll to the top of the screen.

3. **Begin typing the Web address, or *URL (Uniform Resource Locator* for you trivia buffs), on the virtual keyboard that slides up from the bottom of the screen.**

4. **Do one of the following:**

   a. To accept one of the bookmarked (or other) sites that show up on the list, merely tap the name.

   Safari automatically fills in the URL in the address field and takes you where you want to go.

   b. Keep tapping the proper keyboard characters until you've entered the complete Web address for the site you have in mind, and then tap Go at the bottom-right corner of the keyboard.

   It's not necessary to type *www* at the beginning of a URL. So if you want to visit www.theonion.com (for example), typing **theonion. com** is sufficient to transport you to the site in question.

Even though Safari on the iPhone can render Web pages the way they're meant to be displayed on a computer, every so often you may run into a site that will serve up the light, or mobile, version of the Web site, sometimes known as a WAP site. Graphics may be stripped down on such sites. Alas, the producers of these sites may be unwittingly discriminating against you for dropping in on them via a cell phone. Never mind that the cell phone in this case is an iPhone. You have our permission to berate them with letters, e-mails, and phone calls until they get with the program.

I Can See Clearly Now

Now that you know how to open up a Web page, we'll show you how radically simple it is to zoom in on the pages so you can read what you want to read and see what you want to see, without enlisting a magnifying glass.

Try these neat tricks:

✔ **Double-tap the screen so that that portion of the text fills up the entire screen:** It'll take just a second before the screen comes into focus. By way of example, check out Figure 10-3. It shows two views of the same *Sports Illustrated* Web page. In the first view, you see what the page looks like when you first arrive. In the second, you see how the middle column takes over the screen after you double-tapped on it. To return to the first view, double-tap the screen again.

Figure 10-3: Doing a double-tap dance zooms in and out.

- ✐ **Pinch the page:** Sliding your thumb and index finger together and then spreading them apart (or as we like to say, *un-pinching*) also zooms in and out of a page. Again, wait just a moment for the screen to come into focus.

- ✐ **Press down on a page and drag it in all directions, or flick through a page from top to bottom:** You are panning and scrolling, baby.

- ✐ **Rotate the iPhone to its side:** Watch what happens to the White House Web site shown in Figure 10-4. It reorients from portrait to a widescreen view. The keyboard is also wider, making it a little easier to enter a new URL.

Figure 10-4: Going wide.

Opening multiple Web pages at once

When we surf the Web on a desktop PC or laptop, we rarely go to a single Web page and call it a day. In fact, we often have multiple Web pages open at the same time. Sometimes it's because we choose to hop around the Web without closing the pages we've visited. Sometimes a link (see the next section) automatically opens a new page without shuttering the old one. (If they're advertisements, these additional pages aren't always welcome.)

Safari on the iPhone lets you open multiple pages simultaneously. Tap the Pages icon (labeled in Figure 10-1), which is on the right side of the navigation bar at the bottom of the screen, and then tap New Page on the screen that pops up next. Tap the address field and type a URL for your new page.

The number inside the Pages icon lets you know how many pages are open. To see the other open pages, flick your finger to the left or right, as shown in Figure 10-5. Tap a page to have it take over the full screen.

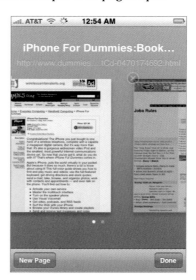

Figure 10-5: All open for business.

To close one of your open Web pages, tap the white X in the red circle, which appears in the upper-left corner of each open page.

Lovable links

Surfing the Web would be a real drag if you had to enter a URL each time you wanted to navigate from one page to another. That's why bookmarks are so useful. And it's why handy links are welcome too. Because Safari functions on the iPhone the same way browsers work on your PC or Mac, links on the iPhone pretty much behave the same way too.

Text links that transport you from one site to another are underlined. Merely tap the link to go directly to that site.

But tapping on some other links leads to different outcomes:

- **Open a map:** Tapping on a map launches the Google Maps application that is, um, addressed in Chapter 12.

- **Prepare an e-mail:** Tap an e-mail address and the iPhone opens the Mail program (see the next chapter), and pre-populates the To field with that address. The virtual keyboard is also summoned so you can add other e-mail addresses and compose a subject line and message.

- **Make a phone call:** Tap a phone number embedded in a Web page, and the iPhone offers to dial it for you. Just tap Call to make it happen, or Cancel to forget the whole thing.

To see the URL for a link, press your finger against the link and keep it there. This is also a way to determine whether a picture has a link.

Not every Web link will cooperate with the iPhone. As of this writing, the iPhone didn't support some common Web standards, notably Adobe Flash video and Java. It's a void we hope is addressed — and Apple can apply such an upgrade (if it so chooses) through a software update. In the meantime, if you come upon an incompatible link, nothing may happen — or a message may be displayed about having to install a plug-in.

Book (mark) 'em, Dano

You already know how useful bookmarks are and how you can synchronize bookmarks from the browsers on your computer. It's equally simple to bookmark a Web page directly on the iPhone:

1. **With the page you want to bookmark open, tap the + at the bottom middle of the screen.**

   The Add Bookmark screen appears, as shown in Figure 10-6, with a default name and folder location.

2. **To accept the default bookmark name and default bookmark folder, tap Save.**

3. **To change the default bookmark name, tap the X in the circle next to the name, enter the new title (using the virtual keyboard), and then tap Save.**

4. **To change the location where the bookmark is saved, tap the > in the Bookmarks field, tap the folder where you want the bookmark kept, and then tap Save.**

Figure 10-6: Turning into a bookie.

To open a bookmarked page after you've set it up, tap the Bookmarks icon at the bottom of the screen (labeled in Figure 10-1), and then tap the appropriate bookmark.

If the bookmark you have in mind is buried inside a folder, tap the folder name first and then tap the bookmark you want.

Altering bookmarks

If a bookmarked site is no longer meaningful, you can change it or get rid of it:

- To remove a bookmark (or folder), tap the Bookmarks icon and then tap Edit. Tap the red circle next to the bookmark you want to toss off the list, and then tap Delete.

- To change a bookmark name or location, tap Edit and then tap the bookmark. The Edit Bookmark screen appears, showing the name, URL, and location of the bookmark already filled in. Tap the fields you want to change. In the Name field, tap the X in the gray circle and then use the keyboard to enter a new title. In the Location field, tap the > and scroll up or down the list until you find a new home for your bookmark.

- To create a new folder for your bookmarks, tap Edit and then tap the New Folder button. Enter the name of the new folder and choose where to put it.

✔ To move a bookmark up or down on a list, tap Edit and then drag the
three bars to the right of the bookmark's name.

Letting History repeat itself

Sometimes you want to revisit a site that you failed to bookmark. But you
can't remember what the darn destination was called or what led you there
in the first place. Good thing you can study the history books.

Safari records the pages you visit and keeps the logs on hand for several
days. Tap the Bookmarks icon, tap History, and then tap the day you think
you hung out at the site. When you find it, tap the listing. You are about to
make your triumphant return.

To clear your history so nobody else can trace your steps — and just what
is it you're hiding, hmmm? — tap Clear at the bottom of the History list.
Alternately, tap Settings on the Home page, tap Safari, and then tap Clear
History. In both instances, per usual, you'll have a chance to back out without wiping the slate clean.

Launching a mobile search mission

Most of us spend a lot of time on the Internet
with search engines. And the search engines
we summon most often are Google and
Yahoo! So it goes on the iPhone.

Although you can certainly use the virtual
keyboard to type **google.com** or **yahoo.com**
in the Safari address field, Apple doesn't
require that tedious effort. Instead, you tap
into Google or Yahoo! via the dedicated
search box shown in Figure 10-7. The default
search engine of choice on the iPhone is
Google, with Yahoo! the first runner-up.

To conduct a Web search on the iPhone, tap
the address field and then tap the Google
(or Yahoo!) search field. Enter your search
term or phrase and then tap the Google (or
Yahoo!) button at the bottom-right of the
keyboard to generate pages of results. Tap
any search results that look promising.

Figure 10-7: Conducting a Google
search about iPhone on the iPhone.

To switch the search box from Google to Yahoo! and vice versa, tap Settings on the Home page, scroll down and tap Safari, tap Search Engine, and then tap to choose one search behemoth over the other.

Saving Web pictures

You can capture most pictures you come across on a Web site (but be mindful of any potential copyright violations depending on what you plan to do with the image). To copy an image from a Web site, press your finger against the image and tap the Save Image button that slides up (along with a Cancel button and sometimes an Open Link button), as shown in Figure 10-8. Saved images end up in your Camera Roll, from which they can be synced back to a computer.

Figure 10-8: Hold your finger against a picture in Safari to save it to the iPhone.

Smart Safari Settings

Along with the riches galore found on the Internet are places in cyberspace where you'll get hassled. Some of you may take pains to protect your privacy and maintain your security.

So return with us now to Settings, by tapping the Settings icon on the Home page. Now tap Safari.

You've already discovered how to change the default search engine and clear the record of the sites you've visited through Settings. Now see what else you can do:

✔ **Clear cookies:** We're not talking about crumbs you may have accidentally dropped on the iPhone. *Cookies* are tiny bits of information that a Web site places on the iPhone when you visit so that Web site will recognize you when you return. You need not assume the worst; most cookies are benign. But if this concept wigs you out, you can do a few things.

Tap Clear Cookies at the bottom of the screen and then tap it again (instead of tapping Cancel). Separately, tap Accept Cookies and then tap Never. Theoretically, you will never receive cookies on the iPhone again. A good middle ground is to accept cookies only from the sites you visit. To do so, tap From Visited. You can also tap Always to accept cookies from all sites.

If you don't set the iPhone to accept cookies, certain Web pages won't load properly.

Tap Safari to return to the main Safari settings page.

- **Clear the cache:** The cache stores content from some Web pages so they load faster the next time you stop by. Tap Clear Cache and then tap Clear Cache again on the next screen to (you guessed it) clear the cache.

- **Turn JavaScript on or off:** This setting is on when the blue On button is showing and off when the white Off button is showing. Programmers use JavaScript to add various kinds of functionality to Web pages, from displaying the date and time to changing images when you mouse over them. However, some security risks have also been associated with JavaScript.

- **Turn plug-ins on or off:** These are typically associated with certain types of video.

- **Block pop-ups:** Pop-ups are those Web pages that show up whether you want them to or not. Often they are annoying advertisements. But at some sites you'll welcome the appearance of pop-ups, so remember to turn blocking off under such circumstances.

- **Developer:** Unless you happen to be a developer, we wouldn't ask you to pay too much attention to this setting. It lets you turn a debug console (showing errors, warnings, tips, logs, and such details that developers find useful) on or off.

Taming Safari is just the start of exploiting the Internet on the iPhone. In upcoming chapters, you discover how to master e-mail, maps, and more.

The E-Mail Must Get Through

hapter 5 shows you how well your iPhone sends SMS text messages. But SMS text messages aren't the iPhone's only written communication trick, not by a long shot. One of the niftiest things your iPhone can do is send and receive real, honest-to-gosh e-mail, using Mail, its modern e-mail application. It's designed not only to send and receive text e-mail messages, but also to handle rich HTML e-mail messages — formatted e-mail messages complete with font and type styles and embedded graphics.

Furthermore, your iPhone can read several types of file attachments, including PDF, Microsoft Word, PowerPoint, and Excel documents, as well as stuff produced through Apple's own iWork software. Better still, all this sending and receiving of text, graphics, and documents can happen in the background, so you can surf the Web or talk to a friend while your iPhone quietly and efficiently handles your e-mail behind the scenes.

Prep Work: Setting Up Your Accounts

First things first. To use Mail you need an e-mail address. If you have broadband Internet access (that is, a cable modem or DSL), you probably received one or more e-mail addresses when you signed up. If you are one of the handful of readers who doesn't already have an e-mail account, you can get one for free from Yahoo! (http://mail.yahoo.com), Google (http://mail.google.com), and many other service providers.

©iStockphoto.com/Chad Anderson

Many (if not all) free e-mail providers add a small bit of advertising at the end of your outgoing messages. If you'd rather not be a billboard for your e-mail provider, either use the address(es) that came with your broadband Internet access (*yourname*@comcast.net, *yourname*@att.net, and so on) or pay a few dollars a month for a premium e-mail account that doesn't tack advertising (or anything else) onto your messages. You can get a me.com e-mail account as part of Apple's $99-a-year MobileMe service.

Set up your account the easy way

Chapter 3 explains the option of automatically syncing the e-mail accounts on your computer with your iPhone. If you chose that option, your e-mail accounts should be configured on your iPhone already. You may proceed directly to the "Darling, You Send Me (E-Mail)" section.

If you have not yet chosen that option but would like to set up your account the easy way now, go to Chapter 3 and read that section, sync your iPhone, and then you, too, may proceed directly to the "Darling, You Send Me (E-Mail)" section.

Set up your account the less easy way

If you don't want to sync the e-mail accounts on your computer, you can set up an e-mail account on your iPhone manually. It's not quite as easy as clicking a box and syncing your iPhone, but it's not rocket science either.

If you have no e-mail accounts on your iPhone, the first time you launch Mail you'll be walked through the following procedure. If you have one or more e-mail accounts on your iPhone already and want to add a new account manually, start by tapping Settings on the Home screen, and then tap Mail, Contacts, Calendars, and Add Account.

Either way, you should now be staring at the Add Account screen, which is shown in Figure 11-1. Proceed to one of the next two sections, depending on your e-mail account.

Figure 11-1: Tap a button to add an account.

Setting up an e-mail account with Yahoo!, Google, AOL, or MobileMe

If your account is with Yahoo!, Google (Gmail), AOL, or Apple's own MobileMe service, tap the appropriate button on the Add Account screen now. If your account is with a provider other than these four, tap the Other button and skip ahead to the next section — that is, with one important exception. If you're setting up company e-mail through Microsoft Exchange, skip the next section and read the one after that.

Enter your name, e-mail address, and password, as shown in Figure 11-2. There's a field for a description of this account (such as work or personal), but it tends to fill in automatically with the same contents in the Address field unless you tell it differently.

Tap the Save button in the top-right corner of the screen. You're finished. That's all there is to setting up your account.

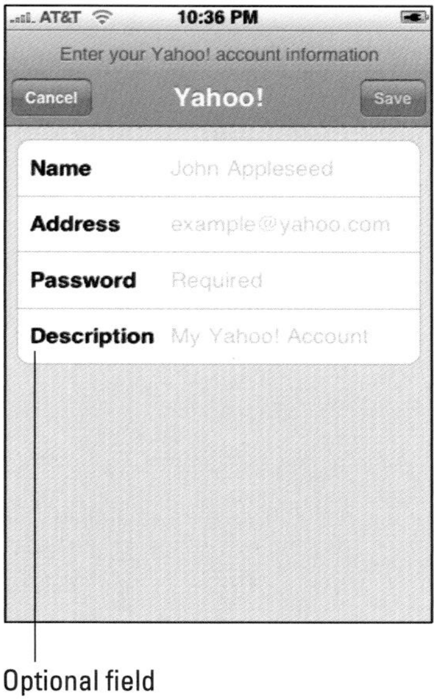

Setting up an account with another provider

If your e-mail account is with a provider other than Yahoo!, Google, AOL, or MobileMe, you have a bit more work ahead of you. You're going to need a bunch of information about your e-mail account that you may not know or have handy.

We suggest that you scan the following instructions, note the items you don't know, and go find the answers before you continue. To find the answers, look at the documentation you received when you signed up for your e-mail account or visit the account provider's Web site and search there.

Optional field

Figure 11-2: Just fill 'em in, tap Save, and you're ready to rock.

Here's how you set up an account:

1. **On the Add Account screen, tap the Other button.**

2. **Fill in the Name, Address, Password, and Description in the appropriate fields, same as if you were setting up a Yahoo!, Gmail, AOL or MobileMe account.**

With any luck, that's all you'll have to do, although you may have to endure a spinning cursor for awhile as the iPhone attempts to retrieve information and validate your account with your provider. Otherwise, continue on with step three.

3. **Tap the button at the top of the screen that denotes the type of e-mail server this account uses: IMAP or POP, as shown in Figure 11-3.**

4. **Fill in the Internet host name for your incoming mail server, which should look something like mail.*provider-name*.com.**

5. **Fill in your username and password.**

6. **Enter the Internet host name for your outgoing mail server, which should look something like smtp.*provider-name*.com.**

   You may have to scroll down to the bottom of the screen to see the outgoing mail server fields.

7. **Enter your username and password in the provided fields.**

8. **Tap the Save button in the upper-right corner to create the account.**

Figure 11-3: If you're not a Yahoo!, Google, AOL, or MobileMe user, you may have a few more fields to fill in before you can rock.

Some outgoing mail servers don't need your username and password. The fields for these items on your iPhone note that they are optional. Still, we suggest that you fill them in anyway. It will save you from having to add them later if your outgoing mail server *does* require an account name and password, which many do these days.

Setting up corporate e-mail

The iPhone has gotten a lot friendlier for business users of late, notably because the device makes nice with the Microsoft Exchange servers that are such a staple in large enterprises.

What's more, if your company supports something known as Microsoft Exchange ActiveSync, you can exploit *"push"* e-mail, so that messages arrive pronto on the iPhone, just as they do on your other computers. For *push* to work, your company must be simpatico with Microsoft Exchange ActiveSync 2003 or 2007.

Setting up Exchange e-mail isn't particularly taxing, although there's a good chance you'll have to consult your employer's IT or tech department for certain settings.

Start out by just touching the Microsoft Exchange icon on the Add Account screen. Fill in what you can: your e-mail address, username (usually as *domain\user*), and password. Or again call on your IT staff for assistance.

On the next screen, shown in Figure 11-4, enter the Server address, assuming Microsoft's Autodiscovery service didn't already find it. That address usually begins with *exchange. company.com*.

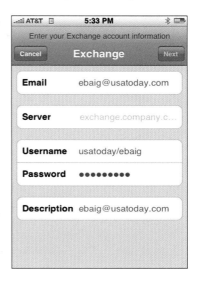

Figure 11-4: You're on your way to a corporate e-mail account.

The company you work for doesn't want just anybody having access to your e-mail — heaven forbid if your phone is lost or stolen. So your bosses may insist that you change the passcode lock inside Settings on the phone. (This is different than the password for your e-mail account.) Skip ahead to Chapter 13 on settings for instructions on adding or changing a passcode. We'll be back here waiting for you. And if your iPhone does end up in the wrong hands, your company can remotely wipe the contents clean.

After your corporate account is fully configured, you have to choose which information you want to synchronize through Exchange. You can choose Mail, Contacts, and Calendars. Tap each one that you want to synchronize through Microsoft Exchange. After you choose an item, you see the blue On button next to it, as shown in Figure 11-5.

Figure 11-5: Keeping Mail, Contacts, and Calendars in sync.

By default, the iPhone keeps e-mail synchronized for three days. To sync for a longer period, head to Settings and tap Mail, Contacts, Calendars, and then tap the Mail account using ActiveSync. Tap Mail Days to Sync and tap No Limit or pick another time frame (1 day, 1 week, 2 weeks, 1 month).

Sorry, but you can configure only one Exchange ActiveSync account per iPhone. If you tap Microsoft Exchange on the Add Account screen of an iPhone that already has an ActiveSync account set up, you'll get no further.

Darling, You Send Me (E-Mail)

Now that your account or accounts are set up, let's look at how to use your iPhone to send e-mail.

Makin' messages

There are several subspecies of messages: pure text, text with a photo, a partially finished message you want to save and complete later (called a draft), a reply to an incoming message, forwarding an incoming message to someone else, and so on. The following sections examine these subsets one at a time.

Sending an all-text message

To compose a new e-mail message, tap Mail on your Home screen. You should see a screen that looks pretty much like the one in Figure 11-6.

Don't worry if yours doesn't look exactly like this or if your folders have different names.

Now, to create a new message, follow these steps:

1. **Tap the New Message button (labeled in Figure 11-6) in the lower-right corner of the screen.**

   A screen like the one shown in Figure 11-7 appears.

Tap to see other e-mail accounts

Number of unread messages

New Message

Name of this e-mail account

Figure 11-6: The mailboxes screen.

2. **Type the names or e-mail addresses of the recipients in the To: field, or tap the + button to the right of To: to choose a contact or contacts from your iPhone's address book.**

3. **(Optional) Tap the field labeled Cc/Bcc/From:. Doing so breaks these out into separate Cc:, Bcc:, and From: fields.** The Cc/Bcc: label stands for *carbon copy/blind carbon copy*. If you haven't used Bcc: before, it enables you to include a recipient on the message that other recipients can't see has been included. It's great for those secret agent e-mails! Tap the respective Cc: or Bcc: field to type in names. Or tap the + that appears in those fields to add a contact. If you tap From instead, you can choose to send the message from any of your e-mail accounts on the fly, assuming, of course, you have more than one account.

Figure 11-7: The New Message screen appears ready for you to start typing the recipient's name.

If you start typing an e-mail address, e-mail addresses that match what you've typed appear in a list below the To: or Cc: field. If the correct one is in the list, tap it to use it.

4. **Type a subject in the Subject field.**

   The subject is optional, but it's considered poor form to send an e-mail message without one.

5. **Type your message in the message area.**

   The message area is immediately below the Subject field.

6. **Tap the Send button in the top-right corner of the screen.**

Your message will wing its way to its recipients almost immediately. If you are not in range of a Wi-Fi network or the AT&T EDGE or 3G data network when you tap Send, the message is sent the next time you are in range of either network.

Sending a photo with a text message

Sometimes a picture is worth a thousand words. When that's the case, here's how to send an e-mail message with a photo enclosed.

Tap the Photos icon on the Home screen and then find the photo you want to send. Tap the button that looks like a little rectangle with a curved arrow springing out of it in the bottom-left corner of the screen, and then tap the Email Photo button.

An e-mail message appears on-screen with the photo already attached; in fact the image appears to be embedded in the body of the message but the recipient will receive it as a regular e-mail attachment. Just address the message and type whatever text you like, as you did for an all-text message in the preceding section, and then tap the Send button.

Saving an e-mail message so you can send it later

Sometimes you start an e-mail message but don't have time to finish it. When that happens, you can save it as a draft and finish it some other time.

Here's how: Start an e-mail message as described in one of the two previous sections. When you're ready to save it as a draft, tap the Cancel button in the top-left corner of the screen. Now tap the Save button if you want to save this message as a draft and complete it another time. If you tap the Cancel button, you cancel the cancel command and go right back to the message and can continue working on it now.

If you tap the Don't Save button, the message disappears immediately without a second chance. Don't tap Don't Save unless you mean it.

To work on the message again, tap the Drafts mailbox. A list of all the messages you've saved as drafts appears. Tap the one you want to work on, and it reappears on the screen. When you're finished, you can tap Send to send it or tap Cancel to save it as a draft again.

The number of drafts appears on the right of the Drafts folder, the same way that the number of unread messages appears on the right of other mail folders such as your Inbox.

Replying to or forwarding an e-mail message

When you receive a message and want to reply to it, open the message and then tap the Reply/Reply All/Forward button, which looks like a curved arrow at the bottom of the screen, as shown in Figure 11-8. Then tap the Reply, Reply All, or Forward button.

The Reply button creates a blank e-mail message addressed to the sender of the original message. The Reply All button creates a blank e-mail message addressed to the sender and all other recipients of the original message. In both cases the subject is retained with a *Re:* prefix added. So if the original subject was *iPhone Tips,* the reply's subject would be *Re: iPhone Tips.*

Tapping the Forward button creates an unaddressed e-mail message that contains the text of the original message. Add the e-mail address(es) of the person or people you want to forward the message to, and then tap Send. In this case, instead of a *Re:* prefix, the subject is preceded by *Fwd:.* So this time the subject would be *Fwd: iPhone Tips.*

You can edit the subject line of a reply or a forwarded message or edit the body text of a forwarded message the same way you would edit any other text. It's usually considered good form to leave the subject lines alone (with the *Re:* or *Fwd:* prefix intact), but there may be times when you want to change them. Now you know that you can.

To send your reply or forwarded message, tap the Send button as usual.

Figure 11-8: Reading and managing an e-mail message.

Settings for sending e-mail

You can customize the mail you send and receive in lots of different ways. In this section, we explore settings for sending e-mail. Later in this chapter, we show you settings that impact the way you receive and read messages. In each instance, you start by tapping Settings on the Home screen. Then:

> ✔ **To hear an alert when you successfully send a message:** Tap the Sound icon on the main Settings screen, and then turn on the Sent Mail setting. If you want to change other settings, tap the Settings button in the top-left corner of the screen. If you're finished setting settings, tap the Home button on the front of your iPhone.

The preceding paragraph is similar for all the settings we discuss in this section and later sections, so we won't repeat them again. To summarize, if you want to continue using settings, you tap whichever button appears in the top-left corner of the screen — sometimes it's called Settings, or Mail, or Accounts, or something else. The point is that the top-left button always returns you to the previous screen so that you can change other settings. And the same applies to pressing the Home button on the front of your iPhone when you're finished setting a setting. That always saves the change you've just made and returns you to the Home screen.

- **To add a signature line, phrase, or block of text to every e-mail message you send:** Tap Settings, tap Mail, Contacts, Calendars, and then tap Signature. (You may need to scroll down to see it). The default signature is _Sent from my iPhone_. You can add text before or after it, or delete it and type something else. Your signature is now affixed to the end of all your outgoing e-mail.

- **To have your iPhone send you a copy of every message you send:** Tap Settings, tap Mail, Contacts, Calendars, and then turn on the Always Cc Myself setting.

- **To set the default e-mail account for sending e-mail from outside the Mail application:** Tap the Settings icon on the Home screen, tap Mail, and then tap Default Account. Tap the account you want to use as the default. For example, when you want to e-mail a picture directly from the Photos application, this designated e-mail account is the one that will be used. Note that this setting applies only if you have more than one e-mail account on your iPhone.

And that's what you need to know about the settings that apply to sending e-mail.

See Me, Read Me, File Me, Delete Me: Working with Messages

The other half of the mail equation is receiving and reading the stuff. Fortunately, you've already done most of the heavy lifting when you set up your e-mail accounts. Getting and reading your mail is a piece of cake.

You can tell when you have unread mail by looking at the Mail icon, in the bottom of your Home screen. The cumulative number of unread messages appears in a little red circle on the top-right of the icon.

Reading messages

To read your mail, tap the Mail icon on the Home screen. The Accounts list appears, and the Inbox in that list displays the number of unread messages in a blue oval to the right of its name.

If you have more than one e-mail account, you may have to tap the Accounts button in the upper-left corner and then choose the appropriate e-mail account before you see the Inbox with the unread messages.

To see the list of unread messages, tap Inbox in the list of mailboxes and then tap a message to read it. When a message is on the screen, buttons for managing incoming messages appear below it (refer to Figure 11-8).

Managing messages

When a message is on your screen, you can do the following in addition to reading it (all buttons are labeled in Figure 11-8):

- ✏ View the next message by tapping the next message button.
- ✏ View the previous message by tapping the previous message button.
- ✏ Check for new messages by tapping the check for new messages button.
- ✏ File this message in another folder by tapping the file message button. When the list of folders appears, tap the folder where you want to file the message.
- ✏ Delete this message by tapping the delete message button. You'll have a chance to cancel in case you tapped the delete message button by mistake.
- ✏ Reply, reply to all, or forward this message (as discussed previously) by tapping the Reply/Reply All/Forward button.
- ✏ Create a new e-mail message by tapping the new message button.

You can delete e-mail messages without opening them in two ways:

- ✏ Swipe left or right across the message and then tap the red Delete button that appears to the right of the message.
- ✏ Tap the Edit button in the upper-left corner of the screen, tap the red minus (–) button to the left of the message, and then tap the red Delete button that appears to the right of the message.

As part of the iPhone 2.0 software upgrade, Apple lets you delete or move messages in bulk. Tap Edit, and then tap the circle to the left of each message you want to delete or move so that a check mark appears. Tap the Delete or Move button at the bottom of the screen shown in Figure 11-9, depending on which action you want to take. Deleted messages are moved to the Trash folder. If you chose Move, tap the new folder in which you want those messages to hang out.

Don't grow too attached to attachments

Your iPhone can even receive e-mail messages with attachments in a wide variety of file formats. What file formats does the iPhone support? Glad you asked.

Here is the list of file formats that your iPhone can receive as attachments, care of Apple:

Figure 11-9: Wiping out, or moving messages, en masse.

- ✓ **Images:** .jpg, .tiff, .gif
- ✓ **Microsoft Word:** .doc and .docx
- ✓ **Microsoft PowerPoint:** .ppt and .pptx
- ✓ **Microsoft Excel:** .xls and .xlsx
- ✓ **Web pages:** .htm and .html
- ✓ **Apple Keynote:** .key
- ✓ **Apple Numbers:** .numbers
- ✓ **Apple Pages:** .pages
- ✓ **Preview and Adobe Acrobat:** .pdf
- ✓ **Text:** .txt
- ✓ **Contact information:** .vcf

If the attachment is a file format not supported by the iPhone (for example, a Photoshop .psd file), you'll see the name of the file but you won't be able to open it on your iPhone.

Here's how to read an attachment:

1. **Open the mail message containing the attachment.**

2. **Tap the attachment (it appears at the bottom of the message so you'll probably need to scroll down to see it).**

   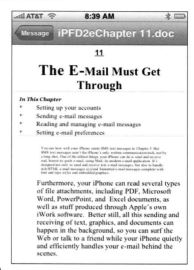

   The attachment, like the one shown in Figure 11-10, downloads to your iPhone and opens automatically.

3. **Read the attachment.**

4. **Tap the Message button in the upper-left corner of the screen to return to the message text.**

More things you can do with messages

But wait! You can do even more with your incoming e-mail messages:

> ✏ To see all the recipients of a message, tap the word Details (displayed in blue) to the right of the sender's name.

Figure 11-10: Text from a Microsoft Word file that was attached to an incoming e-mail message.

> If all recipients are displayed, the word in blue will be Hide rather than Details. Tap it to hide all names but the sender's.

> ✏ To add an e-mail recipient or sender to your contacts, tap the name or e-mail address at the top of the message and then tap either Create New Contact or Add to Existing Contact.

> ✏ To mark a message as unread, tap Mark as Unread, which appears near the top of each message in blue with a blue dot to its left. When you do, the message is again included in the unread message count on the Mail icon on your Home screen and its mailbox and will again have a blue dot next to it in the message list for that mailbox.

> ✏ To zoom in, double-tap the place you want to zoom in on. Double-tap again to zoom out.

> For more precise control over zooming, pinch and un-pinch instead of double-tapping.

✔ To follow a link in a message, tap the link. Links are typically displayed in blue. If the link is a URL, Safari opens and displays the Web page. If the link is a phone number, the Phone application opens and offers to dial the number. If the link is a Map, Maps opens and displays the location. And last but not least, if the link is an e-mail address, a new pre-addressed blank e-mail message is created.

If the link opens Safari, Phone, or Maps, and you want to return to your e-mail, press the Home button on the front of your iPhone and then tap the Mail icon.

Setting your message and account settings

This final discussion of Mail involves more settings that deal with your various e-mail accounts.

Checking and viewing e-mail settings

Several settings affect the way you can check and view e-mail. You might want to modify one or more, so here's what they do and where to find them:

✔ **To set how often the iPhone checks for new messages:** Tap the Settings icon on the Home screen and then tap Fetch New Data. You are entering the world of *fetching* or *pushing*. Check out Figure 11-11 to glance at your options. If your e-mail program supports Push and you have Push turned on (the On button is showing) fresh messages are sent to your iPhone automatically as soon as they hit the server. If you've turned Push off (Off is showing), or your e-mail program doesn't support Push in the first place, the iPhone fetches data instead. Choices for fetching are Manually, Every 15 Minutes, Every 30 Minutes, and Hourly. Tap the one you prefer.

Figure 11-11: Fetch or Push? Your call.

Tap Advanced at the bottom of the screen to determine these Push/Fetch settings for each individual account. Tap the account in question. Push is shown as an option only if the e-mail account you've tapped supports the feature.

As of this writing, Yahoo!, MobileMe (Me.com), and Microsoft Exchange ActiveSync accounts were awfully pushy (but only in a good way).

- **To hear an alert sound when you receive a new message:** Tap the Sounds icon on the main Settings screen and then turn on the New Mail setting.

- **To set the number of recent messages that appears in your Inbox:** Tap the Settings icon on the Home screen, tap Mail, Contacts, Calendars, and then tap Show. Your choices are 25, 50, 75, 100, and 200 recent messages. Tap the number you prefer.

  You can always see more messages in your Inbox regardless of this setting by scrolling all the way to the bottom and tapping Download More.

- **To set the number of lines of each message to be displayed in the message list:** Tap the Settings icon on the Home screen, tap Mail, Contacts, Calendars, tap Preview, and then choose a number. Your choices are 0, 1, 2, 3, 4, and 5 lines of text. The more lines of text you display in the list, the fewer messages you can see at a time without scrolling. Think before you choose 4 or 5.

- **To set the font size for messages:** Tap the Settings icon on the Home screen, tap Mail, Contacts, Calendars, and then tap Minimum Font Size. Your options are Small, Medium, Large, Extra Large, and Giant. Use trial and error to find out which size you prefer. Choose one and then read a message. If it's not just right, choose a different size. Repeat until you're happy.

- **To set whether or not the iPhone shows the To and Cc labels in message lists:** Tap the Settings icon on the Home screen, tap Mail, Contacts, Calendars, and then turn the Show To/Cc Label setting on or off.

- **To turn the Ask Before Deleting warning on or off:** Tap the Settings icon on the Home screen, tap Mail, Contacts, Calendars, and then turn the Ask Before Deleting setting on or off. If this setting is turned on, you need to tap the trash can icon at the bottom of the screen and then tap the red Delete button to confirm the deletion. When it's turned off, tapping the trash can icon deletes the message and you never see a red Delete button.

Altering account settings

The last group of settings we explore deals with your e-mail accounts. Most of you will never need most of these settings, but we'd be remiss if we didn't at least mention them briefly. So here they are, whether you need 'em or not:

- **To stop using an e-mail account:** Tap the Settings icon on the Home screen, tap Mail, Contacts, Calendars, and then tap the account name. Tap the switch to turn off the account.

  This setting doesn't delete the account; it only hides it from view and stops it from sending or checking e-mail until you turn it on again.

- **To delete an e-mail account:** Tap the Settings icon on the Home screen, tap Mail, and then tap the account name. Scroll to the very bottom and tap the red button that says Delete Account. You are given a chance to reconsider. Tap Delete Account if you're sure you want this account blown away or Cancel if you change your mind and want to keep it.

The last settings are somewhat advanced and are all reached the same way: Tap the Settings icon on the Home screen, tap Mail, Contacts, Calendars, and then tap the name of the account you want to work with. Then:

- **To set how long until deleted messages are removed permanently from your iPhone:** Tap Advanced, and then tap Remove. Your choices are Never, After One Day, After One Week, and After One Month. Tap the choice you prefer.

- **To set whether drafts, sent messages, and deleted messages are stored on your iPhone or on your mail server:** Tap Advanced, and then choose the setting (Stored on my iPhone or Stored on the server) for Drafts, Sent Messages, and Deleted Messages. If you choose to store any or all of them on the server, you won't be able to see them unless you have an Internet connection (Wi-Fi, EDGE, or 3G). If you choose to store them on your iPhone, they are always available, even if you don't have Internet access.

We strongly recommend that you not change these next two items unless you know exactly what you're doing and why. If you're having problems with sending or receiving mail, start by contacting your ISP (Internet service provider), e-mail provider, or corporate IT person or department. Then, only change these settings if they tell you to.

- **To reconfigure mail server settings:** Tap Host Name, User Name, or Password in the Incoming Mail Server or Outgoing Mail Server section of the account settings screen and make your changes.

- **To adjust Use SSL, Authentication, IMAP Path settings, or Server Port:** Tap Advanced, and then tap the appropriate item and make the necessary changes.

And that, as they say in baseball, retires the side. You are now fully qualified to set up e-mail accounts and send and receive e-mail on your iPhone.

12

Monitoring Maps, Scrutinizing Stocks, and Watching Weather

In This Chapter

▷ Mapping your route with Maps

▷ Getting quotes with Stocks

▷ Watching the weather with Weather

*I*n this chapter we look at three of the iPhone's Internet-enabled applications: Maps, Stocks, and Weather. We call them *Internet-enabled* because they display information collected over your Internet connection — whether Wi-Fi or wireless data network — in real (or in the case of Stocks, near-real) time.

Maps Are Where It's At

In the first edition of this book we said that the Maps feature was one of the sleeper hits of our iPhone experience and an application we both use more than we expected because it's so darn handy. Since then, Maps has only gotten better and more capable. With Maps, you can quickly and easily discover exactly where you are, find nearby restaurants and businesses, get turn-by-turn driving instructions from any address to any other address, and see real-time traffic information for any location.

©iStockphoto.com/Matt Jeacock

Finding your current location with Maps

Let's start with something supremely simple yet extremely useful — determining your current location. At the risk of sounding like self-help gurus, here's how to find yourself: Tap the Maps icon and then tap the little compass in the lower-left corner.

If you have an iPhone 3G, a pulsating blue marker indicates your location on the map when its GPS is used to find your location (see Figure 12-1). Otherwise, a somewhat larger circle is used to show your approximate location. Either way, when you move around, iPhone can update your location and adjust the map so the location indicator stays in the middle of the screen.

If you tap or drag the map, your iPhone continues to update your location; but it won't re-center the marker, which means that the location indicator can move off the screen.

Finding a person, place, or thing

To find a person, place, or thing with Maps, tap the search field at the top of the screen to make the keyboard appear. Now type what you're looking for. You can search for addresses, zip codes, intersections, towns, landmarks, and businesses by category and by name, or combinations, such as *New York, NY 10022, pizza 60645,* or *Auditorium Shores Austin TX.*

If the letters you type match names in your Contacts list, the matching contacts appear in a list below the search field. Tap a name to see a map of that contact's location. Maps is smart about it, too; it displays only the names of contacts with a street address.

When you finish typing, tap Search. After a few seconds, a map appears. If you searched for a single location, it is marked with a single pushpin. If you searched for a category (*pizza 60645,* for example), you see multiple pushpins, one for each matching location, as shown in Figure 12-2.

So that's how to find just about anything with Maps. Now here's a look at some ways you can use what you find.

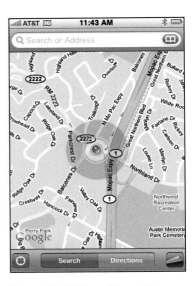

Figure 12-1: With an iPhone 3G, a blue marker shows your GPS location.

Figure 12-2: Search for *pizza 60645* and you see pushpins for all nearby pizza joints.

How does it do that?

Maps uses iPhone's Location Services to determine your approximate location using available information from your wireless data network, local Wi-Fi networks (if Wi-Fi is turned on), and GPS (in iPhone 3G only).

If you're not using Location Services, turning it off will conserve your battery. (Tap Settings, tap General, and then tap Location Services.)

Don't worry if Location Services is turned off when you tap the compass — if so, you'll be prompted to turn it on.

Finally, Location Services may not be available in all areas at all times.

Views, zooms, and pans

First, find out how to work with what you see on the screen. Four views are available at any time: Map, Satellite, Hybrid, and List (Figure 12-2 shows the Map view). Select one view by tapping the curling page button in the lower-right corner. The map then curls back and reveals several buttons, as shown in Figure 12-3.

In Map, Satellite, or Hybrid view, you can zoom to see either more or less of the map — or scroll (pan) to see what's above, below, or to the left or right of what's on the screen:

Figure 12-3: The map curls back to reveal these buttons.

✔ **To zoom out:** Pinch the map or *double-tap using two fingers*. To zoom out even more, pinch or double-tap using two fingers again.

This is a new concept. To double-tap with two fingers, merely tap twice in rapid succession with two fingers rather than the usual one finger. (That's a total of four taps, input very efficiently as two taps per finger.)

✔ **To zoom in:** Un-pinch the map or double-tap (the usual way — with just one finger) the spot you want to zoom in on. Un-pinch or double-tap with one finger again to zoom in even more.

An *un-pinch* is the opposite of a pinch. Start with your thumb and a finger together and then flick them apart.

You can also un-pinch with two fingers or two thumbs, one from each hand, but you'll probably find that a single-handed pinch and un-pinch is handier.

✓ **To scroll:** Flick or drag up, down, left, or right.

Maps and contacts

Maps and contacts go together like peanut butter and jelly. For example, if you want to see a map of a contact's street address, tap the little bookmark icon in the search field, tap the Contacts button at the bottom of the screen, and then tap the contact's name.

Or type the first few letters of the contact's name in the search field and then tap the name in the list that automatically appears below the search field.

After you find a location by typing an address into Maps, you can add that location to one of your contacts. Or you can create a new contact with a location you've found. To do either, tap the location's pushpin on the map, and then tap the little > in a blue circle to the right of the location's name or description (shown next to Gullivers Pizzeria in Figure 12-2) to display its Info screen (see Figure 12-4).

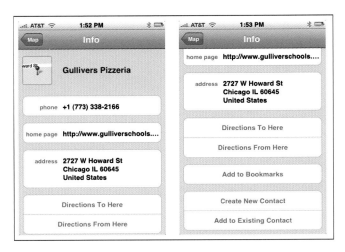

Figure 12-4: The unscrolled Info screen for Gullivers Pizzeria (left), and the same screen when you scroll to the bottom (right).

Now tap either the Create New Contact button or the Add to Existing Contact button on the Info screen. You'll probably have to scroll to the bottom of the Info screen to see these buttons (shown on the right in Figure 12-4).

You work with your contacts by tapping the Contacts icon on your Home screen or tapping the Phone icon on your Home screen and then tapping the Contacts icon at the bottom of the Phone screen.

You can also get driving directions from any location including a contact's address to any other location including another contact's address. You'll see how to do that in the "Smart map tricks" section.

Timesaving map tools: Bookmarks, Recents, and Contacts

Maps offers three tools that can save you from having to type the same locations over and over again. All three appear in the Bookmarks screen, which appears when you tap the little blue bookmark icon that appears on the right side of the search field when it's empty (refer to Figure 12-3).

The fastest way to erase the search field and make the bookmark icon appear is to tap the little *x* on the right, which causes the contents of the search field to disappear instantly.

At the bottom of the Bookmarks screen, you find three buttons: Bookmarks, Recents, and Contacts. The following sections give you the lowdown on these buttons.

Bookmarks

Bookmarks in the Maps application work like bookmarks do in Safari. When you have a location you want to save as a bookmark so that you can reuse it later without typing a single character, tap the little > in a blue circle to the right of its name or description to display the Info screen for that location. Tap the Add to Bookmarks button on the Info screen. (You may have to scroll down the Info screen to see the Add to Bookmarks button.)

You can also drop a pin anywhere on the map by tapping the curling page button in the lower-right corner, and then tapping the Drop Pin button. Once you've dropped a pin you can drag it anywhere on the map. When it's where you want it, tap the pin if you don't see the words Drag To Move Pin above it and Drag To Move Pin and a little > in a blue circle will appear. Tap the little > and the Info screen for the dropped pin appears. Now tap the Add to bookmarks button on the Info screen.

After you add a bookmark, you can recall it at any time. To do so, tap the bookmarks icon in any search field, tap the Bookmarks button at the bottom of the screen, and then tap the bookmark name to see a map of it.

The first things you should bookmark are your home and work addresses and your zip codes. These are things you use all the time with Maps, so you might as well bookmark them now to avoid typing them over and over.

Use zip code bookmarks to find nearby businesses. Choose the zip code bookmark, and then type what you're looking for, such as *78729 pizza, 60645 gas station,* or *90201 Starbucks.*

To manage your bookmarks, first tap the Edit button in the top-left corner of the Bookmarks screen. Then:

- **To move a bookmark up or down in the Bookmarks list:** Drag the little icon with three gray bars that appears to the right of the bookmark upward to move the bookmark higher in the list or downward to move the bookmark lower in the list.

- **To delete a bookmark from the Bookmarks list:** Tap the minus sign to the left of the bookmark's name.

When you're finished using bookmarks, tap the Done button in the top-right corner of the Bookmarks screen to return to the map.

Recents

Maps automatically keeps track of every location you've searched for in its Recents list. To see this list, tap the bookmarks icon in any empty search field, and then tap the Recents button at the bottom of the screen. To see a map of a recent item, tap the item's name.

To clear the Recents list, tap the Clear button in the top-left corner of the screen, and then tap the Clear All Recents button.

When you're finished using the Recents list, tap the Done button in the top-right corner of the screen to return to the map.

Contacts

To see a map of a contact's location, tap the bookmarks icon in any search field, and then tap the Contacts button at the bottom of the screen. To see a map of a contact's location, tap the contact's name in the list.

To limit the Contacts list to specific groups (assuming you have some groups in your Contacts list), tap the Groups button in the top-left corner of the screen and then tap the name of the group. Now only contacts in this group are displayed in the list.

When you're finished using the Contacts list, tap the Done button in the top-right corner of the screen to return to the map.

Smart map tricks

The Maps application has more tricks up its sleeve. Here are a few nifty features you may find useful.

Get route maps and driving directions

You can get route maps and driving directions to any location from any location in a couple of ways:

- ✔ **If there is already a pushpin on the screen:** Tap the pushpin and then tap the little > in a blue circle to the right of the name or description. This action displays the item's Info screen. Now tap the Directions to Here or Directions from Here button to get directions to or from that location, respectively.

- ✔ **When you're looking at a map screen:** Tap the Directions button at the bottom of the map screen. The Start and End fields appear at the top of the screen.

  Type the starting and ending points or choose them from your bookmarks, recent maps, or contacts if you prefer. If you want to swap the starting and ending locations, tap the little swirly arrow button to the left of the Start and End fields.

  When the start and end locations are correct, tap the Route button in the bottom-right corner of the screen and the route map appears, as shown on the left side in Figure 12-5.

  If you need to change the start or end location, tap the Edit button in the top-left corner. If everything looks right, tap the Start button in the top-right corner to receive turn-by-turn driving directions, as shown on the right side in Figure 12-5. To see the next step in the directions, tap the right-facing arrow in the top-right corner; to see the previous step, tap the left-facing arrow in the top-right corner.

Figure 12-5: The route map from Bob's first house in Skokie to Gullivers Pizza in Chicago (left) and the first step in the step-by-step driving directions for that route (right).

If you prefer your driving directions displayed as a list, as shown in Figure 12-6, tap the curling page button in the lower-right corner and then tap the List button.

When you're finished with the step-by-step directions, tap the Search button at the bottom of the screen to return to the regular map screen and single search field.

As well as this works, we wish the iPhone offered the type of audible turn-by-turn directions feature found on some rival GPS devices. You know — where some friendly male or female voice barks out instructions (such as "turn right on Main Street"). Of course, it's entirely possible that Apple or one of its third-party application developers may have added this capability by the time you read this.

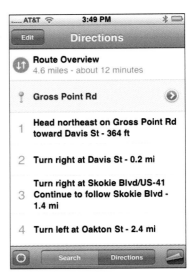

Figure 12-6: Step-by-step driving directions displayed as a list.

Get traffic info in real time

You can find out the traffic conditions for whatever map you're viewing by tapping the curling page button in the lower-right corner and then tapping the Show Traffic button. When you do this, major roadways are color-coded to inform you of the current traffic speed, as shown in Figure 12-7. Here's the key:

- **Green:** 50 or more miles per hour
- **Yellow:** 25 to 50 miles per hour
- **Red:** Under 25 miles per hour
- **Gray:** No data available at this time

Traffic info doesn't work in every location, but the only way to find out is to give it a try. If no color codes appear, assume that it doesn't work for that particular location.

Figure 12-7: Traffic is moving really slow where the road is red, kind of slow where it's yellow, and nice and fast where it's green.

More about the Info screen

If a location has a little > in a blue circle to the right of its name or description (refer to Figure 12-2), you can tap it to see the location's Info screen.

As we explained earlier in this chapter, you can get directions to or from that location, add the location to your bookmarks or contacts, or create a new contact from it, but there are still two more things you can do with a location from its Info screen:

- ✓ Tap its phone number to call it.
- ✓ Tap its URL to launch Safari and view its Web site.

Taking Stock with Stocks

Stocks is another Internet-enabled application on your iPhone. It's a one-trick pony, but if you need its trick — information about specific stocks — it's a winner.

Every time you open the Stocks application by tapping its icon on the Home screen, it displays the latest price for your stocks, with two provisos:

- ✓ The quotes may be delayed by up to 20 minutes.
- ✓ The quotes are updated only if your iPhone can connect to the Internet via either Wi-Fi or a wireless data network.

So tap that Stocks icon and take a peek.

The first time you open Stocks, you see information for the Dow Jones Industrial Average (^DJI), Apple (AAPL), Google (GOOG), Yahoo! (YHOO), and AT&T (T) as the default stocks. Because the chance of you owning that exact group of stocks is slim, this section shows you how to add your own stocks and delete any or all of the default stocks.

Here's how to add a stock:

1. **Tap the *i* button in the bottom-right corner of the initial Stocks screen.**

   The *i* is for *info*.

2. **Tap the + button in the top-left corner of the Stocks screen.**

3. **Type a stock symbol, or a company, index, or fund name.**

4. **Tap the Search button.**

   Stocks finds the company or companies that match your search request.

5. **Tap the one you want to add.**

   Repeat Steps 4 and 5 until you're through adding stocks.

6. **Tap the Done button in the top-right corner.**

And here's how to delete a stock:

1. **Tap the *i* button in the bottom-right corner of the initial Stocks screen.**

2. **Tap the – button to the left of the stock's name.**

3. **Tap the Delete button that appears to the right of the stock's name.**

   Repeat Steps 2 and 3 until all unwanted stocks have been deleted.

4. **Tap the Done button.**

Info button

Figure 12-8: The Stocks screen.

That's all there is to adding and deleting stocks. Figure 12-8 shows my Stocks screen after I deleted one stock and added two others.

Here are a few more things you can do with Stocks. By default, Stocks displays the change in a stock's price in dollars. You can see the change expressed as a percentage in two ways. The easy way is to tap the number next to any stock (green numbers are positive; red numbers are negative). That toggles the display for all stocks. So if they're currently displayed as dollars, tapping any one of them switches them to percent — and vice versa.

The second way to do the same thing takes more steps: Tap the *i* button in the bottom-right corner of the initial Stocks screen. Then tap the % or Numbers button at the bottom of the screen. The numbers are displayed in the manner you choose. Tap the Done button in the top-right corner.

Now refer back to Figure 12-7 and note the chart at the bottom of the window. At the top of the chart, you see a bunch of numbers and letters, namely 1d, 1w, 1m, 3m, 6m, 1y, and 2y. They are buttons you can tap to change the time period shown on the chart. They stand for 1 day, 1 week, 1 month, 3 months, 6 months, 1 year, and 2 years, respectively. Tap one of them and the chart reflects that period of time.

Finally, to look up additional information about a stock at Yahoo.com, first tap the stock's name to select it, and then tap the Y! button in the lower-left corner of the screen. Safari launches and displays the Yahoo.com finance page for that stock, as shown in Figure 12-9.

Figure 12-9: The Yahoo.com finance page for Apple (AAPL).

Weather Watching

Weather is a simple application that provides you with the current weather forecast for the city or cities of your choice. By default, you see a six-day forecast for the chosen city, as shown in Figure 12-10.

If the background for the forecast is blue, as shown in Figure 12-9, it's daytime (between 6:00 a.m. and 6:00 p.m.) in that city; if it's a deep purple, it's nighttime (between 6:00 p.m. and 6:00 a.m.).

To add a city, first tap the *i* button in the bottom-right corner. Tap the + button in the upper-left corner and then type a city and state or zip code. Tap the Search button in the bottom-right corner of the screen. Tap the name of the found city. Add as many cities as you want this way.

To delete a city, tap the *i* button in the bottom-right corner. Tap the red − button to the left of its name, and then tap the Delete button that appears to the right of its name.

You can also choose between Fahrenheit and Celsius by first tapping the *i* button in the bottom-right corner and then tapping either the °F or °C button near the bottom of the screen.

When you're finished, tap the Done button in the top-right corner of the screen.

Figure 12-10: The six-day forecast for Austin, TX.

If you've added more than one city to Weather, you can switch between them by flicking your finger across the screen to the left or the right.

See the three little dots — one white and two gray — at the bottom of the screen in Figure 12-10? They denote the number of cities you have stored (which is three in this case).

Last, but not least, to see detailed weather information about a city at Yahoo.com, tap the Y! button in the lower-left corner of the screen. Safari launches and then displays the Yahoo.com weather page for the current city, as shown in Figure 12-11.

Figure 12-11: Detailed weather on Yahoo.com is just a tap away.

Part V
The Undiscovered iPhone

The 5th Wave By Rich Tennant

"This model comes with a particularly useful function — a simulated static button for breaking out of long-winded conversations."

*T*his part is where we show you what's under the hood and how to configure your iPhone to your liking. Then we look at the things to do if your iPhone ever becomes recalcitrant.

In Chapter 13 we explore every single iPhone setting that's not discussed in depth elsewhere in the book. iPhone offers dozens of different preferences and settings to make your iPhone your very own; by the time you finish with Chapter 13, you'll know how to customize every part of your iPhone that *can* be customized.

We love going on a shopping spree as much as the next guy. Chapter 14 is all about learning to shop in the brand new iPhone App Store, an emporium replete with a gaggle of neat little programs and applications. Best of all, unlike most of the stores you shop in, a good number of the items can be had for free.

iPhones are well-behaved little beasts for the most part, except when they're not. Like the little girl with the little curl, when they're good they're very, very good, but when they're bad, they're horrid. So Chapter 15 is your comprehensive guide to troubleshooting for the iPhone. It details what to do when almost anything goes wrong, offering step-by-step instructions for specific situations as well as a plethora of tips and techniques you can try if something else goes awry. You may never need Chapter 15 (and we hope you won't), but you'll be very glad we put it here if your iPhone ever goes wonky on you.

13

Setting You Straight on Settings

In This Chapter

▶ Taking off in airplane mode

▶ Preparing networks

▶ Finding usage statistics

▶ Seeking sensible sounds and screen brightness

▶ Brushing up on Bluetooth

▶ Tinkering with telephone options

Are you a control freak? The type of person who must have it your way? Boy, have you landed in the right chapter.

Throughout this book we've had an occasion to drop in on Settings, which is kind of the makeover factory for the iPhone. For example, we've come to Settings (by tapping its Home screen icon) to set ringtones, change the phone's background or wallpaper, and specify Google or Yahoo! as the search engine of choice. We've also altered security settings in Safari, tailored e-mail to our liking (among other modifications), and gotten a handle on how to "fetch" or "push" new data.

Settings on the iPhone is roughly analogous to the Control Panel in Windows and System Preferences on a Mac.

Because we covered some settings elsewhere, we won't dwell on every setting here. But there's plenty still to discover to help you make the iPhone your own.

©iStockphoto.com/DSGpro

Sky-High Settings

When you first arrive in Settings, you see the scrollable list shown in Figure 13-1. In all but Airplane Mode (at the very top of the list), a greater-than symbol (>) appears to the right of each listing. This symbol tells you the listing has a bunch of options. Throughout this chapter, you tap the > symbol to check out those options.

If you scroll down to the bottom of the Settings list, you may see settings that pertain to some of the specific third-party apps you've added to the iPhone (as discussed in Chapter 14).

Figure 13-1: Presenting your list of Settings.

Airplane Mode

Using a cell phone on an airplane is a no-no. But there's nothing verboten about using an iPod on a plane to listen to music, watch videos, and peek at pictures. At least, once the craft's reached cruising altitude.

So how do you take advantage of the iPhone's built-in iPod (among other capabilities) while temporarily turning off its phone, e-mail, and Internet functions? By turning on Airplane Mode.

To do so, merely tap Airplane Mode on the Settings screen to display On (rather than Off).

That act disables each of the iPhone's wireless radios: Wi-Fi, Edge, 3G (if applicable), and Bluetooth. While in Airplane Mode, you can't make or receive calls, surf the Web, watch YouTube, or do anything else that requires an Internet connection. The good news is that Airplane Mode keeps your battery running longer — particularly useful if the flight you're on is taking you halfway around the world.

 The appearance of a tiny airplane icon in the status bar at the upper left reminds you that Airplane Mode is turned on. Just remember to turn it off when you're back on the ground.

If you plug the iPhone into an iPod accessory that isn't necessarily compatible because of possible interference from the iPhone's wireless radios, it offers to turn on Airplane Mode for you, as the message displayed in Figure 13-2 indicates.

Wi-Fi

As we've mentioned before, Wi-Fi is typically the fastest wireless network you can use to surf the Web, send e-mail, and perform other Internet tricks on the iPhone.

Figure 13-2: Saying yes to this message may eliminate the static.

You use the Wi-Fi setting to determine which Wi-Fi networks are available to you and which one to exploit based on its signal.

Tap Wi-Fi and all Wi-Fi networks in range are displayed, as shown in Figure 13-3. (Alternatively, you can reach this screen by tapping the General setting, tapping Network, and then tapping Wi-Fi.)

A signal strength indicator can help you choose the network to connect to if more than one is listed; tap the appropriate Wi-Fi network when you've reached a decision. If a network is password-protected, you'll see a lock icon.

You can also turn the Ask to Join Networks setting on or off. Networks that the iPhone is already familiar with are joined automatically, regardless of which one you choose. If the Ask feature is on, you're asked before joining a new network. If it's off, you have to select a network manually.

Figure 13-3: Checking out your Wi-Fi options.

If you've used a particular network automatically in the past but you no longer want your iPhone to join it, tap the > symbol next to the network in question (within Wi-Fi settings) and then tap Forget This Network. The iPhone develops a quick case of very selective amnesia.

In some instances, you have to supply other technical information about a network you hope to glom onto. You encounter a bunch of nasty-sounding terms: DHCP, Boot IP, Static, IP Address, Subnet Mask, Router, DNS, Search Domains, Client ID, HTTP Proxy, and Renew Lease. (At least this last one has nothing to do with real estate or the vehicle you're driving.) Chances are that none of this info is on the tip of your tongue — but that's okay. For one thing, it's a pretty good bet that you'll never need to know this stuff. What's more, even if you *do* have to fill in or adjust these settings, a network administrator or techie friend can probably help you out.

Sometimes, you may want to connect to a network that's closed and not shown on the Wi-Fi list. If that's the case, tap Other and use the keyboard to enter the network name. Then tap to choose the type of security setting the network is using (if any). Your choices are WEP, WPA, WPA2, WPA Enterprise, and WPA2 Enterprise. Again, it's not exactly the friendliest terminology, but we figure that someone nearby can provide assistance.

If no Wi-Fi network is available, you have to rely on 3G or EDGE. If that's not available either, you won't be able to rocket into cyberspace until you regain access to a network.

Settings for Your Senses

The next bunch of settings control what the iPhone looks like and sounds like.

Sounds

Consider Sounds the iPhone's soundstage. Here's where you can turn audio alerts on or off for a variety of functions: new voicemails, new text messages, new mail, sent mail, and calendar alerts. This is also where you set ringtones (as described in Chapter 4).

Other options: You can decide whether you want to hear lock sounds and keyboard clicks. You can determine whether the iPhone should vibrate when you get a call. And you can drag the volume slider to determine how loud your ringer and alerts will be.

There is an alternative: You can use the physical Volume buttons on the side of the iPhone for this purpose, provided you're not already on a call or using the iPod to listen to music or watch video.

Brightening up your day

Who doesn't want a bright, vibrant screen? Alas, the brightest screens exact a tradeoff: Before you drag the brightness slider shown in Figure 13-4 to the max, remember that brighter screens sap the life out of your battery more quickly.

 That's why we recommend tapping the Auto-Brightness control so that it is On. It adjusts the screen according to the lighting conditions around the iPhone while being considerate of your battery.

Wallpaper

Choosing wallpaper is a neat way to dress up the iPhone according to your taste. You can sample the pretty patterns and designs that the iPhone has already chosen for you by tapping the thumbnails shown in Figure 13-5. Of course, although the Mona Lisa is one of your choices, DaVinci may not quite compete with the masterpieces in your own photo albums (more about those in Chapter 9). After making a selection, tap the image and then tap Set Wallpaper.

In General

Certain miscellaneous settings are difficult to pigeonhole. Apple wisely lumped these under the General settings moniker. Here's a closer look.

Figure 13-4: Sliding this control adjusts screen brightness.

Figure 13-5: Choosing a masterpiece background.

About About

You are not seeing double. This section is all about the setting known as About. And About is full of trivial (and not-so-trivial) information *about* the device. What you'll find here is pretty straightforward:

- ✔ **Name of your network.**
- ✔ **Number of songs stored on the device.**
- ✔ **Number of videos.**
- ✔ **Number of photos.**
- ✔ **Storage capacity used and available.** Because of the way the device is formatted, you'll always have a little less storage than the advertised amount of flash memory.
- ✔ **Software version.** We were up to 2.0 as this book was being published. But as the software gets tweaked and updated, your device goes a little beyond. So in parentheses next to the version number, you'll see something like 5A347. That (or another string of numbers and letters) is the build number of the software version you have. It changes when the iPhone's software is updated.
- ✔ **Serial and model numbers.**
- ✔ **Wi-Fi address.**
- ✔ **Bluetooth address.** (More on Bluetooth shortly.)
- ✔ **IMEI and ICCID.** Say what? These stand for the International Mobile Equipment Identity and Integrated Circuit Card Identifier (or Smart Card) numbers. Hey, we warned you some of this was trivial.
- ✔ **Modern *firmware*.** The version of the cellular transmitter.
- ✔ **Legal.** You had to know that the lawyers would get their two cents in somehow. All the fine print is here. And *fine print* it is. Although you can flick to scroll through these lengthy legal notices, you can't pinch the screen to enlarge the text. (Not that we can imagine more than a handful of you will bother to read this legal mumbo-jumbo.)

Using Usage

Think of the Usage setting as one of the places to go on the iPhone for statistics on how you actually employ the device. You get other information in the About setting (under General on the Settings screen), described a little earlier in this chapter.

You can scroll up or down the Usage list to discover the following:

- **The amount of time since you last fully charged your iPhone:** This is indicated in days and hours, both for the time when the iPhone has been unlocked and used and also when it's been locked and in standby mode.
- **Call time:** Shown for the current period and for the lifetime of the product.
- **Cellular Network Data:** The amount of network data you've sent and received over EDGE or 3G. You can reset these statistics by tapping the Reset Statistics button at the bottom of the screen.

Network

There are four major controls under Network settings, one of which, Wi-Fi, we have already addressed. The others are Enable 3G, Data Roaming, and VPN. In this section, we tackle them one by one.

Enable 3G

As you're aware by now, the major benefit of AT&T's 3G network is that it's a lot faster than EDGE (though still not as zippy as Wi-Fi). That said, you're not always going to be carrying the iPhone in a 3G area — and even when you are in coverage, you won't always need to take advantage of faster data speeds. Under these circumstances, tap the Enable 3G button so that Off is showing. Why turn off 3G? The faster network also drains your battery a lot faster. Tap Enable 3G to turn the network back on when you need to.

Of course, the Enable 3G option only turns up on the iPhone 3G.

Data Roaming

You may unwittingly rack up lofty roaming fees when using Safari, exchanging e-mails, and engaging in other data-heavy activities while traveling abroad. Turn off Data Roaming to avoid those excess charges.

FYI on VPN

A *virtual private network,* or VPN, is a way for you to securely access your company's network behind the firewall — using an encrypted Internet connection that acts as a secure "tunnel" for data. The 2.0 version of the iPhone software supports something called Cisco IPSec VPN, which apparently provides the kind of security network administrators want.

iPhone also supports VPN protocols known as *L2TP* (Layer 2 Tunneling Protocol) and *PPTP* (Point-To-Point Tunneling Protocol).

You can configure a VPN on the iPhone by tapping VPN under Network, tapping Add VPN Configuration, and by tapping one of the aforementioned protocols. Then using configuration settings provided by your company, fill in the appropriate server information, account, password, encryption level (if appropriate), and so on. Better yet, lend your iPhone to the techies at the place you work and let them fill in the blanks on your behalf.

After you've configured your iPhone for VPN usage, you can turn that capability on or off by tapping (yep) the VPN On or Off switch inside Settings.

Brushing up on Bluetooth

Of all the peculiar terms you may encounter in techdom, *Bluetooth* is one of our favorites. The name is derived from a tenth-century Danish king named Harald Blåtand, who, the story goes, helped unite warring factions. And, we're told, *Blatand* translates to *Bluetooth* in English. (Bluetooth is all about collaboration between different types of devices, get it?)

Blåtand was obviously ahead of his time. Although we can't imagine he ever dialed a cell phone, today he has an entire short-range wireless technology named in his honor. On the iPhone, you can use Bluetooth to communicate wirelessly with a compatible Bluetooth headset or hands-free car kit. Such optional headsets and kits are made by Apple and many others. They've become more of a big deal as a number of states and municipalities around the U.S. make it illegal to hold a phone up to your mouth and ear to gab while you're driving.

To ensure that the iPhone works with one of these devices, it has to be wirelessly *paired,* or coupled, with the chosen device. With the optional iPhone Bluetooth headset that Apple sells, you can automatically pair the devices by placing the iPhone and headset in a *dual dock* (supplied with the headset), which you connect to your computer.

If you're using a third-party accessory, follow the instructions that came with that headset or car kit so that it becomes *discoverable,* or ready to be paired with your iPhone. Then turn on Bluetooth (under General on the Settings screen) so that the iPhone can find such nearby devices, and the device can find the iPhone. Bluetooth works up to a range of about 30 feet.

You'll know Bluetooth is turned on when you see the Bluetooth icon in the status bar. If the symbol is blue or white, the iPhone is communicating wirelessly with a connected device. (The color differences are to provide contrast to whatever is behind it.) If it's gray, Bluetooth is turned on in the iPhone *but* a paired device is not nearby or is not turned on.

To unpair a device, select it from the device list shown in Figure 13-6 and tap Unpair.

As of this writing, the iPhone's Bluetooth capability was pretty limited compared to what Bluetooth can do on some other devices. It doesn't work with *stereo* Bluetooth headsets. You can't use Bluetooth to exchange files or sync with a computer wirelessly. Nor can you use it to print stuff from the iPhone through a Bluetooth printer. That's because the iPhone does not support any of the Bluetooth *profiles* (or specifications) required to allow such wireless stunts to take place.

Location Services

Location, location, location. Through Maps, through (several) Apps, and by geotagging photos taken with its camera, the iPhone makes good use of knowing where you are. The iPhone 3G exploits its built-in GPS, but even the older-generation iPhone can find your general whereabouts (by *triangulating* signals from Wi-Fi base stations and cellular towers).

Figure 13-6: Falling out of love — unpairing devices.

If that creeps you out a little, don't fret. To protect your right of privacy, individual apps will pop up a quick message (like the one shown in Figure 13-7) asking whether you would like them to use your current location. But you can also turn off Location Services right here in Settings. Not only is your privacy shielded, but you'll also keep your iPhone battery juiced a little longer.

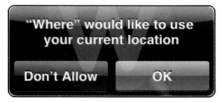

Figure 13-7: This Where app wants to know where you are.

Auto-lock

You can set the amount of time that elapses before the phone automatically locks or turns off the display. Your choices are five minutes before, four minutes before, and so on, all the way down to one minute. Or you can set it so that the iPhone never locks automatically.

If you work for a company that insists on a passcode (see next section), the "Never" Auto-lock option will not be on the list your iPhone shows you.

Don't worry if the iPhone is locked. You can still get calls and text messages and adjust the volume.

Passcode

You can choose a passcode to prevent people from unlocking the phone. Tap Passcode Lock. Then use the virtual keypad to enter a 4-digit code. During this setup, you have to enter the code a second time before it is accepted.

You can determine whether a passcode is required immediately, after 1 minute, after 5 minutes or after 15 minutes. Shorter times are more secure, of course.

You can also change the passcode or turn it off later (unless your employer dictates otherwise), but you need to know the present passcode to apply any changes. If you forget the passcode, you have to restore the iPhone's software, as described in Chapter 15.

One more security setting you'll find in the Change Passcode section: You get to choose whether to show an SMS (text message) Preview or not to show such a Preview.

Restrictions

Parents and bosses may love the new Restrictions settings, but kids and employees usually think otherwise. You can turn on settings to prevent a user from encountering explicit language, using the Safari browser, YouTube, or iTunes, and installing new Apps. When restrictions are in place, the icons for those off-limits functions can no longer be seen.

Stop feeling guilty: You only have users' best interests at heart.

There's no place like the Home button

You can assign one of three shortcuts to double-tapping the Home button. The first, Home, takes you to the Home screen on your iPhone; the second, Phone Favorites, instantly transports you to the Phone Favorites screen; the last, iPod, opens the iPod app. The default is like Dorothy of Kansas . . . if you don't change this setting, double-tapping the Home button will bring you back to the Home screen. Why? Because there's no place like Home. (Groan.)

Finally, switch the iPod Controls setting to On if you want iPod controls to appear when you double-tap the Home button while music is playing.

Date and time

In our neck of the woods, the time is reported as 11:32 PM (or whatever time it happens to be). But in some circles, it's reported as 23:32. If you prefer the latter format on the iPhone's status bar, tap the 24-Hour Time setting (under Date & Time) so that it's On.

This is just one of the settings you can adjust under Date & Time. You can also have the iPhone set the time automatically, using the time reported by the cellular network (and adjusted for the time zone you're in).

If automatic time-setting is turned off, you'll be asked to choose the time zone and then set the date and time manually. Here's how:

1. **Tap Set Automatically so it's Off.**

   You see fields for setting the time zone and the date and time.

2. **Tap the Time Zone field.**

   The current time zone and virtual keyboard are shown.

3. **Tap out the letters of the city or country whose time zone you want to enter until the one you have in mind appears. Then tap the name of that city or country.**

   The Time Zone is automatically filled in for that city.

4. **Tap the Set Date & Time field so that the time is shown. Then roll the bicycle-lock-like controls until the proper time is displayed.**

5. **Tap the date shown so that the bicycle-lock-like controls pop up for the date. Then roll the wheels for the month, day, and year until the correct date appears.**

6. **Tap the Date & Time button to return to the main Date & Time settings screen.**

Keyboard

Under Keyboard settings, you can turn Auto-Capitalization on or off and turn Enable Caps Lock on or off.

Auto-capitalization, which the iPhone turns on by default, means that the first letter of the first word you type after ending a previous sentence with a period, question mark, or exclamation point will be capitalized.

If Cap Locks is enabled, all letters are uppercased LIKE THIS if you double-tap the Shift key. (The Shift key is the one with the arrow pointing north.)

You can also turn on a keyboard setting that inserts a period followed by a space when you double-tap the spacebar. Additionally, you can choose to use an international keyboard (as discussed in Chapter 2), which you choose from the International setting — the very next setting after Keyboard in the General settings area.

Reset

As little kids playing sports, we'd end an argument by agreeing to a "do-over." Well, the Reset settings on the iPhone are one big do-over. Now that we're (presumably) grown up, we're wise enough to think long and hard about the consequences before implementing do-over settings. That said, you may encounter good reasons for starting over; some of these are addressed in Chapter 15.

Here are your reset options:

- **Reset All Settings:** Tapping here resets all settings, but no data or media is deleted.
- **Erase All Content and Settings:** This resets all settings *and* wipes out all your data.
- **Reset Network Settings:** This deletes the current network settings and restores them to their factory defaults.
- **Reset Keyboard Dictionary:** As we pointed out early on, the iPhone's keyboard is intelligent. And one reason it's so smart is that it learns from you. So when you reject words that the iPhone keyboard suggests, it figures the words you specifically banged out ought to be added to the keyboard dictionary. Tapping Reset here removes those added words from the dictionary.
- **Reset Home Screen Layout:** All the icons will be back the way they were at the factory.
- **Reset Location Warnings:** These too will be restored to factory defaults.

Phoning In More Settings

We've already covered most of the remaining settings in previous chapters devoted to e-mail, calendars, the iPod (photos and music), Safari, and e-mail. Still, there are few more we didn't get to — 'til now.

Sorting and displaying contacts

Do you think of us as Ed and Bob or Baig and LeVitus? The answer to that question will probably determine whether you choose to sort your Contacts list alphabetically by last name or first.

Tap Mail, Contacts, Calendars, scroll down to the Contacts section, and peek at Sort Order. Then tap Last, First or First, Last.

You can also determine whether you want to display a first name or last name first. Tap Display Order and then choose First, Last, or Last, First.

Nothing phone-y about these settings

Long ago and far away in Chapter 4, we tipped our hand and indicated that we'd save a few more phone tricks — those found in Phone settings — for this chapter.

So tap Phone now to review some of the choices we didn't get to previously. Be aware that you have to scroll down the screen to find Phone settings.

Call forwarding

If you expect to spend time in an area with poor cell-phone coverage or none at all, you may want to temporarily forward calls to a landline or other portable handset. Here are the simple steps:

1. **On the Settings screen, tap Phone and then tap Call Forwarding.**
2. **Tap to turn on Call Forwarding.**
3. **Use the virtual keypad to enter the number where you want incoming calls to ring.**
4. **Tap the Call Forwarding button to return to the main Call Forwarding screen.**

To change the forwarding number, tap the circle with the X in the phone number field to get rid of the old number, and then enter a new one.

Remember to turn off Call Forwarding to receive calls directly on your iPhone again.

You must have cellular coverage while setting the Call Forwarding feature.

Call waiting

Tap the Call Waiting button to turn the feature on or off. If Call Waiting is off and you are speaking on the phone, the call is automatically dispatched to voicemail.

Displaying Caller ID

Don't want your name or number displayed on the phone you're calling? Make sure to tap Show My Caller ID so it is Off. If privacy isn't a concern, you can leave this setting On.

TTY

Folks who are hearing impaired sometimes rely on a teletype, or TTY, machine, to hold conversations. You can use the iPhone with standard TTY devices by plugging a cable from the TTY device into an optional $19 iPhone TTY adapter and then plugging the adapter into the iPhone. Make sure the TTY setting on the phone is turned On.

Locking your SIM

The tiny SIM (Subscriber Identity Module) card inside your iPhone holds your phone number and other important data. Tap to turn on SIM PIN and enter a password with the keypad. That way, if someone gets hold of your SIM, he or she can't use it in another phone without the password.

If you assign a PIN to your SIM, you have to enter it to turn the iPhone off and on again.

AT&T Services

There's a major difference between the iPhone and all the other Apple products you might buy. That's because you are entering into a relationship not only with Apple but also with the phone company. Tap AT&T Services and then tap any of the following for a shortcut phone call to

- ✔ **Check Bill Balance:** The phone dials *225# and, if all goes according to plan, you receive a text message with the due date and sum owed. Such text messages are not counted against your messaging allotment.

- ✔ **Call Directory Assistance:** The phone dials 411.

✔ **Pay My Bill:** The iPhone dials *729 and you are connected to an automated voice system. You can pay your bill with a checking account, debit card, or credit card by following the voice prompts.

You are billed for phone service *from AT&T,* not Apple. Of course, charges for any music or other content purchased in iTunes from your computer are paid to Apple through whichever credit card you have on file, as with any iPod.

✔ **View My Minutes:** This time *646# is called. You again receive a text reply that doesn't count against your messaging allotment.

✔ **Voice Connect:** The iPhone dials *08 to connect you to automated news, weather, sports, quotes, and more. Just bark out the kind of information you're looking for, such as "finance," and follow voice prompts for stock quotes, business news, and so on. Or say "sports" and follow voice prompts to get the latest scores of your favorite team.

Not all AT&T Services make a phone call. If you tap the AT&T MyAccount button, Safari opens an AT&T account management page on the Web.

We trust that you control freaks are satisfied with all the stuff you can manage inside Settings. Still, the iPhone may not always behave as you want. For the times when things get *out* of control, we highly recommend Chapter 15.

Apply Here (to Find Out About iPhone Apps)

*O*ne of the best things about the iPhone these days is that you can download and install applications created by so-called "third parties," which is to say not created by Apple (the first party) or you (the second party). At this writing, hundreds of applications are available; by the time you read this there will no doubt be thousands. Some are free, others cost money; some are useful, others are lame; some are perfectly well-behaved, others quit unexpectedly (or worse). The point is that a lot of apps are available — and some are better than others.

You can obtain and install applications for your iPhone in two ways:

⮕ On your computer
⮕ On your iPhone

To use the App Store on your iPhone, it must be connected to the Internet. And if you obtain an app on your computer, it won't be available on your iPhone until you sync it with your computer.

But before you can use the App Store on your iPhone *or* your computer, you first need an iTunes Store account. So if you don't already have one, we suggest you launch iTunes on your computer and choose Store⇨Create Account to set one up.

Let's put it this way: If you don't have an iTunes Store account, you won't be able to download a single cool app for your iPhone. 'Nuff said.

Using Your Computer to Find Apps

Okay, start by finding cool iPhone applications using iTunes on your computer. Follow these steps:

1. **Launch iTunes.**

2. **Click the iTunes Store in the source list on the left.**

App Store (NEW)

3. **Click the App Store link.**

   The iTunes App Store appears as shown in Figure 14-1.

How to look for apps from your computer

Now that you've got the iTunes App Store on your screen, you have a couple of options for exploring its virtual aisles. Allow us to introduce you to the various "departments" available from the main screen.

Browsing the App Store screen

The main departments are featured in the middle of the screen, and ancillary departments appear on either side of them. Let's start with the ones in the middle:

✔ The New department has eight visible icons (Vicinity to Shazam in Figure 14-1) representing apps that are (what else?) new.

There are only eight icons visible, but the New department actually has more than that. Look to the right end of the title bar for each department shown down the center section of the screen. Notice the little arrow inside a circle and the words *See All?* Click the See All link to show *all* the apps in that department on a single screen. Or, you can click the little arrow inside a circle on the left or right edge of the departments to see another screen full (eight more in the case of the New department) of icons. Finally, the little dots in the middle of the title bar for each department tell you how many screens that department contains (three in the case of the New department).

iTunes Store (in souce list)

App Store link

Search iTunes Store

Figure 14-1: The iTunes App Store in all its glory.

- The What's Hot department features eight icons (SmugShot to PayPal in Figure 14-1) representing apps that are popular with other iPhone users.

- The Staff Favorites department shows eight icons (although you can see only the first four — Critter Crunch to Phone Saber — and a tiny bit of the tops of the next four in Figure 14-1) of apps that are highly recommended by the iTunes Store staff.

Apple has a habit of redecorating the iTunes Stores every so often, so allow us to apologize in advance if things don't look or act exactly as described here.

There are also display ads for six featured apps between the New and What's Hot departments (Texas Hold 'em to Jott for iPhone).

The little dots in the middle of the title bars of these departments — three dots for the New and What's Hot departments and two dots for Staff Favorites — tell you how many screens of additional apps are available. And the little arrows on the left and right sides of the departments let you navigate to these additional screens.

Two other departments appear to the right of the main ones: Top Paid Apps, and one of our favorite departments, Top Free Apps. The number-one app displays both its icon and its name; the next nine apps show text links only.

Finally, to the left of the main departments is a special navigation department known as Categories, with text links to describe each one. Click these links to see the available apps that fit each category description.

Using the Search field

Browsing the screen is great, but if you know exactly what you're looking for we have good news and bad news. The good news is that there's a faster way. Just type a word or phrase into the Search iTunes Store field in the upper-right corner of the main iTunes window, as shown in Figure 14-2, and then press Enter or Return to initiate the search.

Figure 14-2: I'd like to be able to use my iPhone as a flashlight, so I searched for the word *flashlight*.

The bad news is that you have to search the entire iTunes Store, which includes music, television shows, movies, and other stuff in addition to iPhone apps.

Ah, but there's more good news: Your search results are segregated into categories — one of which is Applications, as shown in Figure 14-2. And here's even more good news: If you click the See All link at the right end of the Application category's title bar, all iPhone applications that match your search word or phrase appear.

Getting more information about an app

Now that you know how to find apps in the App Store, this section delves a little deeper and shows you how to find out more about an application that interests you.

Checking out the detail screen from your computer

To find out more about an application icon, featured app, or text link on any of the iTunes App Store screens, just click it. A detail screen like the one shown in Figure 14-3 appears.

Figure 14-3: The detail screen for Tap Tap Revenge, a nifty little free game that's kind of like Guitar Hero for your iPhone.

This screen should tell you most of what you need to know about the application, such as basic product information and a narrative description, what's new in this version, the language it's presented in, and the system requirements to run the app.

Bear in mind that the application description on this screen was written by the application's developer and may be somewhat biased. Never fear, gentle reader; in the next section we show you how to find reviews of the application — written by people who have actually used it.

Notice that this application is rated 4+, as you can see below the Get App button near the top of Figure 14-3. That means that this app contains no objectionable material. Here are the other possible ratings:

- **9+:** May contain mild or infrequent occurrences of cartoon, fantasy, or realistic violence; or infrequent or mild mature, suggestive, or horror-themed content that may not be suitable for children under the age of 9.

- **12+:** May contain infrequent mild language; frequent or intense cartoon, fantasy, or realistic violence; mild or infrequent mature or suggestive themes; or simulated gambling that may not be suitable for children under the age of 12.

- **17+:** May contain frequent and intense offensive language; frequent and intense cartoon, fantasy, or realistic violence; mature, frequent and intense mature, suggestive, or horror-themed content; sexual content; nudity; depictions of alcohol, tobacco, or drugs that may not be suitable for children under the age of 17. You must be at least 17 years old to purchase games with this rating.

One other feature of the detail pages is worth mentioning, and that is the collection of useful links below the application description. In Figure 14-3, these links include Tapulous Web Site, Tap Tap Revenge Support, All Applications By Tapulous, Tell A Friend, and so on. We urge you to explore these links at your leisure.

Reading reviews from your computer

If you scroll down the detail screen, near the bottom you'll find a series of reviews by the app's users (you can't actually see these reviews in Figure 14-3). Each review includes a star rating, from zero to five. If an app is rated four or higher, it's a pretty good indication that the application is well liked by people who own it.

If you could scroll down the screen shown in Figure 14-3, you'd see that this application has an average rating of four-and-a-half stars based on 1,041 user reviews. You'd also see three or four recent reviews with their star ratings. And if you care to read even more reviews, you can click the See All Reviews link.

Downloading an app

This part is simple. When you find an application you'd like to try, just click its Get App button. At that point, you have to log in to your iTunes Store account, even if the application is free.

After you've logged in, the application begins downloading. When it's finished, the app appears in the Applications section of your iTunes Library, as shown in Figure 14-4.

Downloading an application to your iTunes Library is only the first half of getting it onto your iPhone. After you download an app, you have to sync your iPhone before the application will be available on it.

Updating an app

Every so often the developer of an iPhone application releases an update. Sometimes these updates add new features to the application, sometimes they squash bugs, and sometimes they do both. In any event, updates are usually a good thing for you and your iPhone, so it makes sense to check for them every so often. To do this using iTunes, click the Check for Updates link near the bottom-right corner of the Applications screen, which you can see in Figure 14-4.

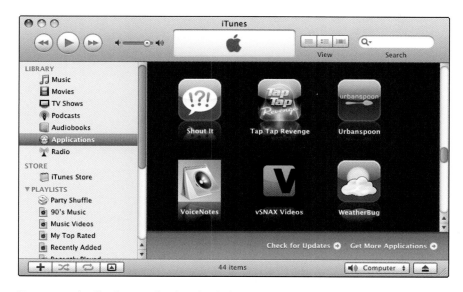

Figure 14-4: Applications you've downloaded appear in the Applications section of your iTunes Library.

If you click the Get More Applications link next to the Check for Updates link, you'll find yourself back at the main screen of the iTunes App Store, as shown in Figure 14-1.

Using Your iPhone to Find Apps

Finding apps with your iPhone is almost as easy as finding them using iTunes. The only requirement is that you have an Internet connection of some sort — Wi-Fi or wireless data network — to browse, search, download, and install apps.

To get started, tap the App Store icon on your iPhone's Home screen.

When you launch the App Store, you'll see five icons at the bottom of the screen, representing five ways to interact with the store, as shown in Figure 14-5.

Figure 14-5: The icons across the bottom represent the five sections of the App Store.

How to look for apps from your iPhone

The first three icons at the bottom of the screen — Featured, Categories, and Top 25 — offer three ways to browse the virtual shelves of the App Store.

Browsing the iPhone App Store

The Featured section has two tabs at the top of the screen: New (shown in Figure 14-5) and What's Hot. These two tabs represent two different pages full of apps.

The Top 25 section works the same way. Its two tabs — Top Paid and Top Free — represent pages of popular apps that either cost money (paid) or don't (free).

Each page displays roughly 20–25 apps, but you see only four or five at a time on the screen. So remember to flick up or down if you want to see the others.

The Categories section works a little bit differently. It has no tabs and its main page contains no apps. Instead it offers a list of categories such as

Books, Games, Lifestyle, Utilities, and so on. Tap a category to see a page full of apps of that type.

Using the Search icon

If you know exactly what you're looking for, instead of simply browsing you can tap the Search icon and type a word or phrase.

Getting more information about a particular application

Now that you know how to find apps in the App Store, the following sections show you how to find out more about a particular application.

Checking out the detail screen from your iPhone

To learn more about any application on any page, tap it, and a detail screen like the one shown in Figure 14-6 appears.

Remember that the application description on this screen was written by the developer and may be somewhat biased.

Oddly enough, as of this writing, only the 17+ rating appears on a detail page. The other age ratings (4+, 9+, and 12+), discussed in the earlier section "Checking out the detail screen from your computer," don't appear.

Reading reviews from your iPhone

Scroll down to the bottom of any detail screen, and you find a star rating for that application. It's also the link to that application's reviews; tap it to see a page full of them. At the bottom of that page is another link called More Reviews. Tap it to see (what else?) more reviews.

Figure 14-6: This is the detail screen for Remote, a free application from Apple that lets you control iTunes or AppleTV from your iPhone.

Downloading an App

To download an application to your iPhone, tap the price button near the top of its detail screen. In Figure 14-6, it's the blue thing that says Free. You may or may not be asked to type your iTunes Store account password before the App Store disappears and you're taken to the Home screen page where the new application's icon resides. The new icon appears, slightly dimmed, with the word *Loading* beneath it and a blue progress indicator near its bottom, as shown in Figure 14-7.

By the way, if the app happens to be rated 17+, you see a warning screen after you type your password. You have to click the OK button to confirm that you're over 17 before the app downloads.

The application is now on your iPhone, but it won't be copied to your iTunes library on your Mac or PC until your next sync. If your iPhone suddenly loses its memory (unlikely), or if you delete the application from your iPhone before you sync (as described later in this chapter), that application is gone forever.

After you download an app to your iPhone, the next time you sync your phone you'll see a dialog box that informs you: "iTunes has found purchased items on the iPhone that are not present in your iTunes library. Do you want to transfer these items from this iPhone back to your iTunes library? If you do not transfer these purchased items to your iTunes library they will be removed from your iPhone." Your options are Transfer or Don't Transfer. Click one.

Progress bar

Figure 14-7: This application is being downloaded; here the blue progress bar indicates that it's about one-third done.

By the way, although the dialog box refers to "purchased items," you'll see it even if the application was a freebie.

If an application is less than10MB in size, you can download it directly to the iPhone through the 3G cellular network or Wi-Fi. Larger programs require Wi-Fi or require you to sync up through iTunes on your PC or Mac.

Updating an app

As mentioned earlier in the chapter, every so often the developer of an iPhone application releases an update. To check for updates using the App Store on your iPhone, tap the Updates icon at the bottom of the screen.

If you see (in the middle of the screen) a message that says, "All Apps are Up-to-date," none of the apps on your iPhone will require an update at this time. If an app needs updating, it appears with an Update button next to it. Tap the button to update the application. If more than one application needs updating, you can update them all at once by tapping the Update All button at the bottom of the screen.

If you try to update an application purchased from another iTunes Store account, you are prompted for that account's ID and password. If you can't provide them, you won't be allowed to download the update.

Working with Applications

That's almost everything you need to know about installing third-party applications on your iPhone. However, you might find it helpful to know how to delete, review, or report a problem with an app.

Deleting an app

You can delete an application in two ways: In iTunes on your computer or right from your iPhone.

To delete an application in iTunes, click Applications in the source list, and then either

✔ Click the application's icon to select it and then choose Edit⇨Delete.

Or

✔ Right-click (Control+click on a Mac) the application's icon and choose Delete.

Either way, you see a dialog box asking whether you're sure you want to remove the selected application. If you click the Remove button, the application is removed from your iTunes library, as well as from any iPhone that syncs with your iTunes library.

Here's how to delete an application on your iPhone:

1. **Press and hold on any icon until all the icons begin to "wiggle."**

2. **Tap the little "x" in the upper-left corner of the application you want to delete, as shown in Figure 14-8.**

   A dialog box appears, informing you that deleting this application will also delete all its data.

3. **Tap the Delete button, as shown in Figure 14-8.**

Little Xes

Delete button

Figure 14-8: Tap an application's little *x*, and then tap Delete to remove it from your iPhone.

If you've synced your iPhone since you downloaded the application and transferred it to your iTunes library, deleting it from your iPhone won't get rid of it permanently. The next time you sync, it will return to your iPhone like a bad penny. To get rid of it for good, you have to remove it from your iTunes library.

Writing an app review

Sometimes you love or hate an application so much that you want to tell the world about it. In that case, you should write a review. You can do this in two ways: In iTunes on your computer or right from your iPhone.

To write a review using iTunes, follow these steps:

1. **Navigate to the detail page for the application in the iTunes App Store.**

2. **Scroll down the page to the Reviews section and click the Write a Review link.**

   You may or may not have to type your iTunes store password at this point.

3. **Click the button for the star rating you want to give the application (1 to 5).**

4. **In the Title field, type a title for your review.**

5. **In the Review field, type your review.**

6. **Click the Preview button when you're finished.**

The Preview screen appears. If the review looks good to you, click the Submit button. If you want to add something or edit it, click the Edit button. If you decide not to review the app after all, click the Cancel button.

To write a review from your iPhone, follow these steps:

1. **Tap the App Store icon to launch the App Store.**

2. **Navigate to the detail screen for the application.**

3. **Scroll down the page to the Reviews item and tap it.**

 4. **From the Reviews screen, tap the New Document icon.**

5. **Tap the Write a Review button.**

   You may or may not have to type your iTunes store password at this point.

6. **Tap one to five of the dots at the top of the Submit Review screen to rate the application.**

7. **In the Title field, type a title for your review.**

8. **In the Review field, type your review.**

9. **Tap the Send button in the upper-right corner of the screen.**

Whichever way you submit your review, Apple will review your submission. As long as it doesn't violate the (unpublished) rules of conduct for app reviews, it will appear in a day or two in the App Store, in the Reviews section for the particular application.

Reporting a problem

Every so often you get an app that's recalcitrant — a dud that doesn't work properly, crashes, freezes, or otherwise messes up your iPhone. When this happens, you should definitely report the problem so that Apple and the developer know of the problem and (hopefully) can fix it.

We're beginning to sound like parrots here, but once again, you can do this two ways: In iTunes on your computer or right from your iPhone.

Here's how to report a problem with an app from iTunes:

1. **Launch iTunes, choose Store⇨Sign In, type your account name and password, and then click the Sign In button.**

2. **Choose Store⇨View My Account.**

3. **Click the Purchase History button (even if the application was free).**

4. **Click the Report a Problem button at the bottom of the Purchase History screen.**

5. **Click the arrow to the left of the application that has the problem.**

6. **Click the Report a Problem link for the application that has the problem.**

7. **Choose a problem from the Problem drop-down menu. If your problem isn't listed, choose "My concern isn't listed here" and write about the problem in the Comments field.**

8. **Click the Submit button.**

Frankly, we think it's a bit easier to report a problem with an app from your iPhone. Here's how to do that:

1. **Tap the App Store icon to launch the App Store.**

2. **Navigate to the detail screen for the application.**

3. **Scroll down the page to the Reviews item and tap it.**

4. **From the Reviews screen, tap the New Document icon.**

5. **Tap the Report a Problem button.**

   You may or may not have to type your iTunes store password at this point.

6. **Tap one of the three buttons to identify the type of problem you're reporting:** *This application has a bug; This application is offensive*; **or** *My concern is not listed here.*

7. **Type your report in the Comments field.**

8. **Tap the Report button in the upper-right corner of the screen to submit the report.**

And there you have it — you now know everything you need to know to find, install, delete, review, and report problems with iPhone applications!

As Steve Jobs is so fond of saying in his keynotes, there is one last thing. . . . In a few pages (Chapter 16 to be precise), we tell you about ten of our favorite iPhone apps to kick off the famous Part of Tens.

When Good iPhones Go Bad

In This Chapter

▷ Fixing iPhone issues

▷ Dealing with network and calling problems

▷ Eliminating that sinking feeling when you can't sync

▷ Perusing Apple's Web site and discussion forums

▷ Sending your iPhone to an Apple Store

*1*n our experience, iPhones are usually reliable devices. And most users we've talked to have reported trouble-free operation. Notice our use of the word *most*. That's because every so often, a good iPhone goes bad. It's not a common occurrence, but it does happen. So in this chapter we look at the types of bad things that can happen, along with suggestions for fixing them.

What kind of bad things are we talking about here? Well, things such as

©iStockphoto.com/Jonathan Maddock

✏ Problems with the phone itself

✏ Problems making or receiving calls

✏ Problems with wireless networks

✏ Problems with synchronization, computers (both Mac and PC), or iTunes

After all the troubleshooting, we tell you how to get even more help if nothing we've suggested does the trick. And finally, if your iPhone is so badly hosed that it needs to go back to the mothership for repairs, we offer ways to survive the experience with a minimum of stress or fuss.

iPhone Issues

Our first category of troubleshooting techniques applies to an iPhone that is frozen or otherwise acting up. The recommended procedure when this happens is to perform the six Rs in sequence. What are the six Rs? Glad you asked. They are

- Recharge
- Restart
- Reset your iPhone
- Remove your content
- Reset settings and content
- Restore

So if your iPhone acts up on you — if it freezes, won't wake up from sleep, won't do something it used to do, or in any other way acts improperly — don't panic; this section describes the things you should try, in the order we (and Apple) recommend you try them.

If the first technique doesn't do the trick, go on to the second. If the second one doesn't work, try the third. And so on.

Recharge

If your iPhone acts up in any way, shape, or form, the first thing you should try is to give its battery a full recharge.

Don't plug the iPhone's dock connector–to–USB cable into a USB port on your keyboard, monitor, or USB hub. You need to plug it into one of the USB ports on your computer itself. That's because USB ports on your computer supply more power than the other ports.

You can use the included USB power adapter to recharge your iPhone from an AC outlet rather than from a computer.

Restart

If you recharge your iPhone and it still misbehaves, the next thing to try is restarting it. Just as restarting a computer often fixes problems, restarting your iPhone sometimes works wonders.

Here's how to restart:

1. **Press and hold the Sleep/Wake button.**

2. **Slide the red slider to turn the iPhone off, and then wait a few seconds.**

3. **Press and hold the Sleep/Wake button again until the Apple logo appears on the screen.**

4. **If your iPod is still frozen, misbehaves, or doesn't start, press and hold the Home button for 6 to 10 seconds to force any frozen applications to quit, and then perform Steps 1 to 3 again.**

If this doesn't get your iPhone back up and running, move on to the third *R*, resetting your iPhone.

Reset your iPhone

To reset your iPhone, merely press and hold the Sleep/Wake button and then press and hold the Home button on the front. When you see the Apple logo, release both buttons.

Resetting your iPhone is like forcing your computer to restart after a crash. Your data shouldn't be affected by a reset — and in many cases it will cure whatever was ailing your iPhone. So don't be shy about giving this technique a try. In many cases, your iPhone will be back to normal after you've reset it this way.

Remember to press and hold the Sleep/Wake button *before* you begin to press and hold the Home button. If you press both at the same time, you'll create a screen shot — a picture of whatever is on your screen at the time — instead of resetting your iPhone. (Such screen pictures, by the way, are stored in the Photos app's Camera Roll. Find out more about this feature at the end of Chapter 18.)

Unfortunately, sometimes resetting *doesn't* do the trick. When that's the case, you have to take stronger measures.

Remove content

Up to now, nothing you've done should have taken more than a minute or two. We hate to tell you, but that's about to change. Because the next thing you should try is removing some or all of your data to see whether perhaps it's the cause of your troubles.

To do so, you'll need to sync your iPhone and reconfigure it so that some or all of your files are *not* synchronized (which will remove them from the phone). The problem could be contacts, calendar data, songs, photos, videos, or podcasts. If you suspect a particular data type — for example, you suspect your photos because whenever you tap the Photos icon on the Home screen your iPhone freezes — try removing that data first.

Or, if you have no suspicions, uncheck every item and then sync. When you're finished, your iPhone should have no data on it.

If that fixed it, try restoring your data, one type at a time. If the problem returns, you have to keep experimenting to determine which particular data type or file is causing the problem.

If you're still having problems, the next step is to reset your iPhone's settings.

Reset settings and content

This is actually two steps: The first one, resetting your iPhone settings, resets every iPhone *setting* to its default — the way it was when you took it out of the box. Resetting the iPhone's settings doesn't erase any of your data or media. The only downside is that you may have to go back and change some settings afterwards. So this is a step you can try without trepidation. To do it, tap the Settings icon on your Home screen, and then tap General, Reset, and Reset All Settings.

Be careful *not* to tap Erase All Content and Settings, at least not yet. Erasing all content takes more time to recover from (because your next sync takes a long time), so you should try Reset All Settings first.

Now, if resetting all settings didn't cure your iPhone, you have to try Erase All Content and Settings. You'll find it in the same place as Reset All Settings (tap Settings, General, Reset).

This will delete everything from your iPhone — all of your data, media, and settings. Because all these things are stored on your computer — at least in theory — you should be able to put things back the way they were with your next sync. But you will lose any photos you've taken, as well as contacts, calendar events, and On-the-Go playlists you've created or modified since your last sync.

After using Erase All Content and Settings, check to see whether your iPhone works properly. If it doesn't cure what ails your iPhone, the final *R* is restoring your iPhone using iTunes.

Restore

Before you give up the ghost on your poor, sick iPhone, you can try one more thing. Connect your iPhone to your computer as though you were about to sync. But when the iPhone appears in the iTunes source list, click the Restore button on the Summary tab. This will erase all of your data and media, and reset all your settings as well.

Because all of your data and media still exist on your computer (except for photos you've taken, contacts, calendar events, and On-the-Go playlists you've created or modified since your last sync, as noted previously), you shouldn't lose anything by restoring. Your next sync will take longer than usual, and you may have to reset settings you've changed since you got your iPhone. But other than those inconveniences, restoring shouldn't cause you any additional trouble.

Okay. So that's the gamut of things you can do when your iPhone acts up. If you tried all this and none of it worked, skim through the rest of the chapter to see whether anything else we recommend looks like it might help. If not, your iPhone probably needs to go into the shop for repairs.

Never fear, gentle reader. Be sure and read the last section in this chapter, "If Nothing We Suggested So Far Helped." Your iPhone may be very sick, but we'll help ease the pain by sharing some tips on how to minimize the discomfort.

Problems with Calling or Networks

If you're having problems making or receiving calls, problems sending or receiving SMS text messages, or problems with Wi-Fi or your wireless carrier's data network, this section may help. The techniques here are short and sweet — except for the last one, restore. Restore, which we describe in the previous section, is still inconvenient and time consuming, and it still entails erasing all your data and media and then restoring it.

But first, here are some simple steps that may help. Once again, we suggest you try them in this order (and so does Apple).

1. **Check the cell signal icon in the top-left corner of the screen.**

   If you don't have at least one or two bars, you may not be able to use the phone or SMS text-message function.

2. **Make sure you haven't left your iPhone in Airplane Mode, as described in Chapter 13.**

   In Airplane Mode, all network-dependent features are disabled, so you can't make or receive phone calls, send or receive SMS text messages, or use any of the applications that require a Wi-Fi or data network connection (that is, Mail, Safari, Stocks, Maps, and Weather).

3. **Try moving around.**

   Changing your location by as little as a few feet can sometimes mean the difference between four bars and zero bars, or being able to use a Wi-Fi or wireless data network or not. If you're inside, try going outside. If you're outside, try moving ten or twenty paces in any direction. Keep an eye on the cell signal or Wi-Fi icon as you move around, and stop when you see more bars than you saw before.

4. **Turn on Airplane Mode by tapping Settings on the Home screen and then tapping the Airplane Mode On/Off switch to turn it on. Wait 15 or 20 seconds and then turn it off again.**

Toggling Airplane Mode on and off like this resets both the Wi-Fi and wireless data-network connections. So if your network connection was the problem, toggling Airplane Mode on and off may very well correct it.

5. **Restart your iPhone.**

If you've forgotten how, refer to the "Restart" section a few pages back. As we mentioned, restarting your iPhone is often all it takes to fix whatever was wrong.

6. **Make sure your SIM card is firmly seated.**

A SIM (Subscriber Identity Module) card is a removable smart card used to identify mobile phones. It allows users to change phones by moving the SIM card from one phone to another.

To remove the SIM card, use the included SIM-eject tool (if you have an iPhone 3G), or find a very fine-gauge paper clip, straighten one end, and then stick the straight end *gently* into the hole on the SIM tray, as shown in Figure 15-1.

When the SIM tray slides out, carefully lift out the SIM card and then reinsert it, making sure it's firmly situated in the tray before you *gently* push the tray back in until it locks.

Figure 15-1: Removing the SIM tray.

If none of the preceding fixed your network issues, try restoring your iPhone as described previously in the "Restore" section.

Performing a restore deletes everything on your iPhone — all of your data, media, and settings. You should be able to put things back the way they were with your next sync. If that doesn't happen, for whatever reason, you can't say we didn't warn you.

Sync, Computer, or iTunes Issues

Our last category of troubleshooting techniques applies to issues that involve synchronization and computer/iPhone relations. If you're having problems syncing or your computer doesn't recognize your iPhone when you connect it, here are some things to try.

Once again, we suggest that you try these procedures in the order they're presented here.

1. **Recharge your iPhone.**

   If you didn't try it previously, try it now. Go back to the "iPhone Issues" section at the beginning of the chapter and read what we said about recharging your iPhone. Every word there also applies here.

2. **Try a different USB port or a different cable if you have one available.**

   It doesn't happen often, but occasionally USB ports and cables go bad. When they do, they invariably cause sync and connection problems. So it's always a good idea to make sure that a bad USB port or cable isn't to blame.

   If you don't remember what we've said about using USB ports on your computer rather than the ones on your keyboard, monitor, or hub, we suggest you reread the "Recharge" section, earlier in the chapter.

3. **Restart your iPhone and try to sync again.**

   We describe restarting in full and loving detail in the "Restart" section, earlier in the chapter.

4. **Reinstall iTunes.**

   Even if you have an iTunes installer handy, it's probably a good idea to visit the Apple Web site and download the latest and greatest version, just in case. You'll always find the latest version of iTunes at www. apple.com/itunes/download/.

More Help on the Apple Web Site

If you've tried everything suggested so far and are still having problems, don't give up just yet. Here are a few more places you may find help. We recommend that you check out some or all of them before you throw in the towel and smash your iPhone into tiny little pieces (or ship it back to Apple for repairs, as described in the next section).

First, Apple offers an excellent set of support resources on its Web site at `www.apple.com/support/iphone`. You can browse support issues by category, search for a problem by keyword, or use the iPhone Troubleshooting Assistant to resolve common problems, as shown in Figure 15-2.

Troubleshooting Assistant link

Figure 15-2: Apple's iPhone support pages offer several kinds of helpful information.

We wouldn't advise putting a lot of hope in the Troubleshooting Assistant. If you've tried everything we've suggested in this chapter, then you've probably tried everything the Troubleshooting Assistant will suggest. However, since it's easier to update a Web site than it is to update a book, the Troubleshooting Assistant could offer techniques we didn't know when we wrote this. So, although it may just repeat things you already know, it could also have something new. Give it a try.

While you're visiting the Apple support pages, another section could be helpful: the discussion forums. You'll find them at `http://discussions.apple.com`, and they're chock-full of questions and answers from other iPhone users. It's been our experience that if you can't find an answer to a support question elsewhere, you can often find something helpful in these forums. You can browse by category (Integrating iPhone into your Digital Life, for example, in Figure 15-3) or search by keyword.

Either way, you'll find thousands of discussions about almost every aspect of using your iPhone. Better still, frequently you can find the answer to your question or a helpful suggestion.

Figure 15-3: Page 1 of 177 pages of discussions about integrating the iPhone into your digital life.

Now for the best part: If you can't find a solution by browsing or searching, you can post your question in the appropriate Apple discussion forum. Check back in a few days (or even in a few hours) and some helpful iPhone user may very well have replied with the answer. If you've never tried this fabulous tool, you're missing out on one of the greatest support resources available anywhere.

Last, but certainly not least, before you give up the ghost you might want to try a carefully worded Google search. It couldn't hurt and you might just find the solution you've spent hours searching for.

If Nothing We Suggested So Far Helped

If you've tried every trick in the book (this one) and still have a malfunctioning iPhone, it's time to consider shipping it off to the iPhone hospital (better known as Apple, Inc.). The repair will be free if your iPhone is still under its one-year limited warranty.

You can extend your warranty to up to two years from the original purchase date if you want. To do so, you need to buy the AppleCare Protection Plan for your iPhone. You don't have to do it when you buy the phone, but you must buy it before your one-year limited warranty expires. The cost is $69.

Here are a few things you should know before you take your phone in to be repaired:

- *Your iPhone will be erased during its repair,* so you should sync your iPhone with iTunes before you take it in, if you can. If you can't, and you've entered data on the phone since your last sync, such as a contact or an appointment, the data won't be there when you restore your iPhone upon its return.

- Remove any third-party accessories such as a case or screen protector.

- Remove the SIM card from your iPhone (as described in the "Problems with Calling or Networks" section) and keep it in a safe place.

Do not, under any circumstances, forget this step. Apple will not guarantee that your SIM card will be returned to you after a repair. If you do forget this step, Apple suggests that you contact your local AT&T store and obtain a new SIM card with the proper account information. Ouch.

Although you may be able to get your iPhone serviced by AT&T or by mail, we recommend that you take it to your nearest Apple Store for two reasons:

- ✔ **No one knows your iPhone like Apple.** One of the geniuses at the Apple Store may be able to fix whatever is wrong without sending your iPhone away for repairs.

- ✔ **Only the Apple Store offers an Advance Replacement plan for iPhones needing repairs.** The AppleCare Advance Replacement Service costs $29 plus tax when your iPhone is under warranty or covered by the AppleCare Protection Plan. This service provides you with a new iPhone before you have to send in your old one for service.

If your iPhone *isn't* under warranty or AppleCare, you can still take advantage of the Advance Replacement Service but it'll cost you a lot more — $228 (8GB) or $328 (16GB) plus tax as of this writing.

If you choose the AppleCare Advance Replacement Service, you won't have to activate the new phone, and it will have the same phone number as the phone it replaces. All you need to do is pop your old SIM card into the new phone, sync it with iTunes to fill it with the data and media files that were on your sick iPhone, and you're good to go.

Part VI
The Part of Tens

*I*t's written in stone somewhere at Wiley world headquarters that we *For Dummies* authors must include a Part of Tens in every single *For Dummies* book we write. It is a duty we take quite seriously. So in this part, you'll find a list of ten of our favorite applications plucked from the iPhone App Store. These include programs to turn your iPhone into a capable Internet radio, a couple of really addictive games, and even an app to help you find a place to eat. We then move on to our diverse collection of ten fabulous Web resources every iPhone user should know about. We tell you about online destinations to practice typing on iPhone's multitouch display, calculate tips, and compile a shopping list. Even your very fortune awaits you in these next few pages.

We close the show with one of our favorite topics: hints, tips, and shortcuts that make life with your iPhone even better. Among the ten, you discover how to look at the capacity of your newly-favored device in different ways, find out how to share Web pages, and pick up another trick or two on using iPhone's virtual keyboard.

Ten Appetizing Apps

*K*iller app is familiar jargon to anyone who has spent any time around computers. It refers to an application so sweet or so useful that just about everybody wants or must have it.

You could make the argument that the most compelling killer app on the iPhone is the very App Store we expound on in Chapter 14. This online emporium has an abundance of splendid programs — dare we say killer apps in their own right? — many of which are free. These cover everything from social networking tools to entertainment. Okay, so there are some rotten apples in the bunch too. But we're here to accentuate the positive.

With that in mind, we offer an arbitrary list of 10 favorite apps. But we encourage you to keep poking around for your own killer programs.

©iStockphoto.com/David Spieth

Pandora

We've long been fans of Pandora on the computer. So we're practically deliri-ous that this custom Internet radio service is available *gratis* on the iPhone.

It works on the phone in much the same way it does on a PC or Mac. You type in the name of a favorite musician or song title and Pandora creates an instant personalized radio station with selections that exemplify the style you chose. Figure 16-1 shows some of the eclectic stations we created. Tapping Quick Mix plays musical selections across all your stations. Tapping the + brings up the iPhone keyboard so that you can add a new station.

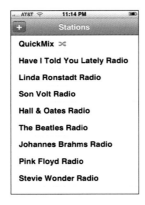

Figure 16-1: Eclectic online radio stations from Pandora.

Say you type **Beatles.** Pandora's instant Beatles station will include perfor-mances from John, Paul, George, and Ringo, as well as tunes from other acts.

And say you type in a song title, such as *Have I Told You Lately.* Pandora will construct a station with similar music after you tell it whether to base tunes on the Van Morrison, Rod Stewart, or other rendition.

Pandora comes out of the Music Genome Project, an organization of musicians and technologists who analyze music according to hundreds of attributes (melody, harmony, vocal performances, and so on).

You can help fine-tune the music Pandora plays by tapping the thumbs-up or thumbs-down icon below the album cover of the song being played, as shown in Figure 16-2.

If you tap the triangular-icon you can bookmark the song or artist being played — or head to iTunes to purchase it directly on the phone (if available).

Tap for explanation of why song is playing

Tap to return to station list

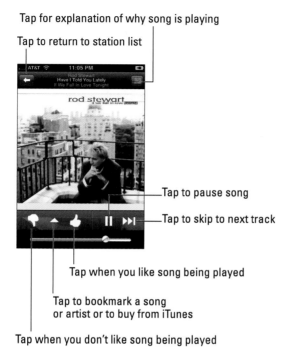

Tap to pause song

Tap to skip to next track

Tap when you like song being played

Tap to bookmark a song
or artist or to buy from iTunes

Tap when you don't like song being played

Figure 16-2: Have we told you lately how much we like Pandora?

AOL Radio

Whereas Pandora is all about creating your own fresh radio stations on the fly, AOL Radio is about playing regular stations that already exist. These include AOL's own Internet radio stations, broken out by genre, and more than 150 terrestrial radio stations owned by CBS Radio.

If you tap the Locals icon, the iPhone looks for stations in the very area in which you are listening, using GPS, cellular or Wi-Fi to determine your whereabouts. But you can also pick stations in some other locale, letting a New Yorker, say, listen to a station in St. Louis, or more than two dozen other locations.

When you stumble upon a station you really like, tap the star in the upper-right corner of the screen to add it to your list of favorites. Then just tap Favorites to find the station later. Or tap Recents to return to stations you recently took in.

Of course, you need Internet access to be able to hear these stations.

Midomi Mobile

Hum a few bars and fake it. That's precisely what you'll find yourself doing with the appealing Midomi Mobile app from Melodis Corp. You hum a melody into the iPhone. Midomi attempts to name that tune.

More often than not, in our tests, it did — Midomi correctly identified "Hotel California," "Yesterday," "Smile," and "People," among other songs in our humming repertoire. And while Midomi didn't properly ID every song, every time — it couldn't possibly be because we were, gulp, humming out of tune — the program still earned our respect.

You can bolster Midomi's accuracy by humming 10 seconds or longer.

There are other ways to identify a song via Midomi. You can say the name of a song or artist, type in a search, or hold your iPhone up to the radio when a song is playing (see Shazam, later in this chapter).

Just tap the appropriate Sing, Say, Grab, or Type icon at the bottom of the screen to search a song or artist by your method of choice. When you make a match, you can jump to YouTube videos or purchase the track in iTunes.

For us, though, the most fun was hearing other people hum the very songs we did. We'll pass no judgment on their musical talents (and hope they return the favor).

Urbanspoon

You're looking for a place to eat in an unfamiliar city. Or maybe you're just bored with the same old haunts in your own neck of the woods. Either way, Urbanspoon can help you find a place to dine serendipitously.

Figure 16-3: Hungering for a new place to eat?

As Figure 16-3 shows, Urbanspoon's screen looks something like a Las Vegas slot machine with three spinning wheels. The first wheel represents the neighborhood you might eat in. The second designates a food type (Ethiopian, Indian, Tacos, you name it). And the third gives you a rough idea of how much eating in some joint is going to cost you, using a scale of one to four $ signs.

When you literally shake the iPhone (or, alternatively, tap the Shake button), the wheels spin until they land on a random restaurant. Tap the little circle with the right-pointing arrow for the address and phone number of the chosen restaurant. You can tap on the number to call it. Or tap More Info to check out any reviews.

If the choice exceeds your budget or doesn't meet your dietary standards — what do you mean you don't want donuts for dinner? — merely shake the iPhone and try again. You can press one or more of the little lock icons under each spinning wheel to filter your restaurant search by a given criteria.

With your permission, Urbanspoon uses the iPhone's GPS or other location-finding smarts to find a nearby restaurant. Or you can direct a search manually from a list of more than 60 cities. Best of all, Urbanspoon is free.

Crash Bandicoot Nitro Kart 3D

We admit it — we're suckers for racing games. Vivendi Games Mobile's Crash Bandicoot is pretty darn addictive, although you will have to fork over ten bucks. The challenge is to steer your race car through a dozen colorful tracks by tilting the phone to activate the iPhone's accelerometer motion sensor.

If you have trouble, tap Options from the main Crash Bandicoot menu and tap Accelerometer to adjust the sensitivity.

If you're a video-game newbie or find yourself in desperate need of an iPhone Driver's Ed course, we recommend tapping Tutorial under the Start Game menu. It offers helpful hints as you race, as shown in Figure 16-4.

Figure 16-4: Hoping to avoid crashing in Crash.

The game is rated 4+, meaning parents can safely let their kids have at it.

Shazam

Ever heard a song on the radio or television and wondered what it was called or who was singing it? With Shazam you may never have to wonder again. Just launch Shazam and hold your iPhone near the source of the music and in a few seconds the song title and artist's name will magically appear on your iPhone screen, as shown in Figure 16-5.

Figure 16-5: Point your phone at the music (left) and Shazam tells you the artist, title, and more (right).

In Shazam parlance, that song has now been *tagged*. Now if tagging were all Shazam could do, that would surely be enough. But wait, there's more . . . after Shazam tags a song you can

- Buy the song at the iTunes store
- Watch related videos on YouTube
- Take a picture and attach it to a tag
- E-mail a tag to a friend

It isn't great at identifying classical music or opera, nor is it adept at identifying obscure indie bands (or, as with Midomi, picking up on humming). But if you use it primarily to identify popular music, Shazam is amazing. It even worked in a noisy airport terminal. And you can't beat the price: Shazam is free.

Remote

Leave it to Apple to come up with one of the coolest iPhone apps money can't buy (because it's free). It's called Remote, and it lets you control music playing in iTunes on your computer, Apple TV, or AirPort Express.

With Remote, you can use your iPhone to do almost everything you can do in iTunes: Play, pause, skip, shuffle, search, or browse your iTunes library. Better yet, you can do it from anywhere in your house that has Wi-Fi.

Because the interface is almost exactly the same as the iPod application on your iPhone, you already know how to use it. (If you need help with the iPod function on your iPhone, see Chapter 7.)

Remote is free, but it does require a couple of basics: a computer running Apple's iTunes software and a Wi-Fi network.

MotionX Poker Dice

MotionX Poker is a five-card poker game played by rolling five dice. Each hand pits you against the dealer and gives you three chances (rolls) to make the best hand, as shown on the left in Figure 16-6.

You roll the dice by shaking your iPhone, which is a cool use of your iPhone's accelerometer. Combine that with the superb sound effects and judicious use of your iPhone's ability to vibrate, and the experience is quite realistic.

Increasing your chip count unlocks beautiful new dice sets (as shown on the right in Figure 16-6), new tables, commemorative gems, and more.

Figure 16-6: (Left) My last roll and three aces so far. . . .
(Right) The more you win, the more dice you get to choose from.

The only bummer is that the version of the game available when we wrote this froze up occasionally. If that happens, you can tap the Home button to exit the game and then tap the MotionX Poker icon to restart it — and things pick up where you left off. While this bug has never affected our iPhones' functionality, it is annoying, especially in a game that's otherwise enjoyable and polished. With any luck, the developer will have squashed the bug before you read this.

Even so, the game is very pretty, lots of fun, and way more addicting than you might expect such a simple game to be. In spite of the occasional hiccups, we can't seem to stop playing. MotionX Poker Dice is $4.99 (and worth it).

Tap Tap Revenge

Are you a fan of the Guitar Hero or Rock Band console games? If so, you'll love the free Tap Tap Revenge game. The object is to tap musical "beats," which appear as colored dots hurling toward you. Tap them as they pass over the white line near the bottom of the screen to score points. When an arrow appears, tilt the iPhone in that direction to score. Figure 16-7 shows a game in progress.

Figure 16-7: The game thinks I'm doing great, so it must be true.

Tap Tap Revenge is a lot like those more expensive games, but you can play it anytime and anywhere. Alas, you have only a very limited number of songs available. And unlike the repertoire in Guitar Hero or Rock Band, we guarantee you've never heard of any of the songs or artists.

Even so, it's free and it's a lot of fun. We think you'll find yourself playing again and again as you try to beat your high score. Now, if you'll excuse us, we've got beats to tap.

Box Office

We like movies, so we use the Box Office app a lot. Feed it your zip code and then browse local theatres by movie, show time, rating, or distance from your current location. Another nice feature is the capability to buy tickets to most movies from your iPhone with just a few additional taps.

There are other free movie apps out there, but we like Box Office best for its clean interface and ratings from RottonTomatoes.com. Oh, and Box Office is free. What a concept.

Ten Terrific Web Resources

*A*ll through this book you've heard us rave about how great the iPhone Internet experience is. But you can't have a great experience without some great Web sites to visit. And so here are ten Web sites that will make your iPhone even more useful or fun.

If you type faster on your computer than on your iPhone, bookmark these sites on your computer and then sync those bookmarks with your iPhone. And if you have more than a few iPhone-specific bookmarks, create an iPhone bookmark folder on your computer and put all of them into it. Then the next time you sync, that bookmark folder will appear on your iPhone, making it easy to use all of your favorite iPhone sites.

©iStockphoto.com/Missing35mm

Wi-Fi Hotspot Finder Extraordinaire

Sure, you can use the Maps application to find a Wi-Fi hotspot in a pinch. Just tap Maps, then type *hotspot* and the zip code you want to search. Assuming that zip code has some Wi-Fi hotspots, a map full of pushpins appears. But Maps doesn't discern between free hotspots and the ones you have to pay for. And Maps doesn't offer a review of the hotspot's signal quality. Although Maps is plenty easy to use, we know an ever better, easier way. It's called JiWire Wi-Fi Finder, and it has a clean interface that makes it easy to search for hotspots in more than 150,000 locations in 135 countries. It also allows you to limit your search to free hotspots, as shown in Figure 17-1.

After you download the application and tap the Go button, a list of hotspot locations appears. Tap the name of a found hotspot, and you see another screen with its name, address, phone number, and three buttons: Call, Map, and Info. The Call and Map buttons do what you'd expect: dial the phone number and display the location in the Maps application, respectively. But the Info button is the best; it tells you more about the business and the quality of its wireless network.

Figure 17-1: JiWire Wi-Fi Finder is a better way to find Wi-Fi hotspots.

JiWire Wi-Fi Finder is easy to use, it's elegant, it does stuff Maps doesn't, and best of all, it's free. How can you not love that? Go to `http://iphone.jiwire.com`.

iPhone News, Tips, and More

We've long had enormous respect for our tech brethren at CNet Networks. And the folks over there have created a comprehensive Web resource called iPhone Atlas, with news, troubleshooting tips, and discussion groups surrounding your prized possession. User forums tackle a gaggle of iPhone-related issues: the legality of unlocking an iPhone, how to send pictures via SMS, how to handle voicemail setup problems, to name just a few.

iPhone Atlas is simply laid out, even if it's hardly the prettiest site we've ever seen. And while we're quibbling, we'd have preferred to be able to access the full HTML iPhone Atlas site on our phones' Safari browsers, rather than the lighter mobile-oriented version of the site.

Still, iPhone Atlas is chock-full of the kind of information that iPhone junkies can't seem to get enough of. Start at `http://www.iphoneatlas.com`.

Fast, Easy Shopping with OneTrip Shopping List

No matter how good of an iPhone typist you are, we have a faster, easier way to make shopping lists. It's called OneTrip Shopping List. Rather than typing items for a list, you tap them. Here's how it works:

1. **Tap a category (see Figure 17-2 left).**

2. **Tap an item or items in the category (see Figure 17-2 middle).**

3. **At the store, tap each item as you toss it into your shopping cart and a check mark magically appears next to its name (see Figure 17-2 right).**

Figure 17-2: First tap a category (left), then tap an item or items in that category (middle) to create a OneTrip Shopping List (right).

You can edit a list any time you like, and you can type any item not included in one of the categories. With another tap, you can e-mail the list to yourself or anyone you want. OneTrip Shopping List has one last great feature — it's free. Go to `http://onetrip.org/onetrip/`.

Calculating Tips Has Never Been Easier

Sure you can use the iPhone's calculator to figure out how much of a tip to leave, but using Danny Goodman's Tip Calculator, at `http://dannyg.com/iphone/tipCalc`, is a whole lot easier. Just tap the Food & Bevs or Tax field and a numeric keypad pops up on the screen.

Specify the number of diners and the amounts for food and tax, and the Tip Calculator does the rest by calculating the gratuity, total, and total amount per diner, as shown in Figure 17-3.

If you tap the little *i* to the left of Gratuity, you can even choose how the tip is calculated — as a percent of the food and beverage total or as a multiple of the sales tax.

Figure 17-3: Specify the number of diners and the amount of food, drink, and tax; the Tip Calculator does the rest.

Tip Calculator, like the other items in this chapter, is 100% free of charge, leaving you extra cash to be a generous tipper.

Match Three Gems

Bejeweled, at `www.popcap.com`, is a free Web version of PopCap's bestselling "match three gems" game. If you've ever played Bejeweled on the Mac or PC, or JewelToy on the Mac, you know exactly how Bejeweled works on the iPhone.

For those unfamiliar with these enjoyable and addictive games, the goal is to arrange three or more matching gems in a line either horizontally or vertically. To move the gems, you tap one, and then tap any adjacent gem to swap their places, as shown on the left in Figure 17-4.

A swap occurs only if doing so will form a line of three or more matching gems. In Figure 17-4, swapping the purple triangle and the yellow diamond creates a vertical line of three purple triangle gems. The three purple gems disappear, as shown in the figure, and you score 10 points!

New gems fall from the top of the board to fill in any gaps. If you create gaps lower in the board, gems slide downward to fill them, and new gems fall from the top. The more lines of three or more gems you make, the higher your score. The game ends when no more lines of three or more matching gems can be created.

Tap

Tap

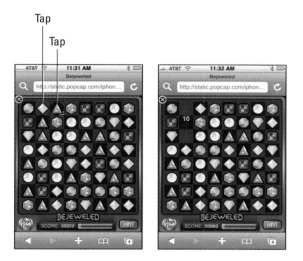

Figure 17-4: (Left) You've created a row of three purple triangles.
(Right) The three purple triangles disappear, and you score 10 points!

It's simple, mindless fun, but more addictive than you might think. Games only take a few minutes and you can't beat the price (free).

By the way, if you find you enjoy this game, you'll probably like Bejeweled 2 even better. It has exclusive features like Power Gems and Hyper Cubes and is available in the iTunes App Store for $9.99.

Practice Typing

By now, you've probably done a fair share of typing using the iPhone's multi-touch keyboard. Some of you may still be struggling with it. For others, let's just say you're getting a tad cocky. "Look at me. I'm hot stuff. This keyboard thing is really a piece of cake."

Think so? Why not put your skills to the test? That's what the iPhone Typing Test site (`http://www.iphonetypingtest.com/`) is all about. You can try your hand, um, fingers at two types of tests.

In the first test, your goal is to type a sentence as quickly and accurately as possible. The sentence appears in a yellow box at the top of the screen. The test begins when you tap inside the blue field just below the yellow field. At that moment, the sentence you are trying to match and the virtual keyboard appear simultaneously.

When you are finished typing, tap Done to see how you fared, as shown in Figure 17-5. Are you still feeling cocky?

The second exam is a freestyle test in which you get to type anything you want for as long as you want. When you tap Done, your words-per-minute are calculated. Before leaving the site, check out the typing tips section.

Figure 17-5: You get to see how fast — and accurate — you are.

An Instant Messaging Workaround

We were surprised that instant messaging was among the features Apple left out when the iPhone was launched. Apple has long included a fine IM program called iChat on Macs. And IM is a popular feature on some rival cell phones.

Apple may well add a version of iChat on the iPhone, possibly even by the time you read this. But if they haven't gotten around to it yet, check out JiveTalk from BeeJive (`http://iphone.beejive.com/`).

The site was still in a beta testing stage as this book was being prepared, but you could already head there and log onto your existing AOL Instant Messenger (AIM), Google Talk, ICQ, Jabber, MSN Messenger, or Yahoo Messenger account.

It's easy to set up these accounts so that they'll work through JiveTalk. Tap the + button at the JiveTalk Home screen, and then tap the downward arrow next to the Network field to choose an IM network from the list that appears at the bottom of the screen. Tap Done and enter your username and password. If you so choose, tap the Save Account check box so you don't have to enter this information every time you want to engage in an IM session.

You can log into all your IM accounts at the same time. Your compadres across all your accounts appear in one integrated buddy list; a little icon next to a name indicates which IM account each person is associated with. A virtual keyboard slides up from the bottom the moment you tap the text box to type a message to a buddy. The actual IM dialog appears in text bubbles.

Through the JiveTalk's settings, you can choose whether or not to display offline buddies, show status messages, and display emoticons (smiley faces and the like).

There is an official AOL/AIM chat application available in the iTunes App Store, but we have found JiveTalk more responsive, more stable, and just plain better behaved.

One last thing: The BeeJive folks are working on a BeeJive iPhone application you can use instead of this Web application. By the time you read this, it may be available at the iTunes App Store (price unknown at press time).

Wassup with Widgets?

Some people refer to useful Web sites or applications for your iPhone as *widgets*. If you're looking for a widget — from a handy little periodic table of the elements to a cheap gas finder, or whatever — one of the most comprehensive widget lists we've found is the iPhone Widget List, at `http://iphone widgetlist.com/`.

Listed apps carry user ratings and status updates. You also can tap a See It Now button to get a closer peek at the widget.

iPhone Network Speed Tester

Ever wonder if your Internet connection — Wi-Fi or EDGE — is faster or slower than average? If so, you're going to enjoy using the iPhone Network Test at `http://www.iphonenetworktest.com/`. Just tap the Start Test link on the front page, and after a few seconds your network speed appears, as shown on the left in Figure 17-6.

Kbps (kilobits per second) is a common measure of your data transfer rate. A kilobit is 1,000 bits, so one kilobit per second equals 1,000 bits per second.

If you tap the link for EDGE, 3G, or Wi-Fi (which you can't see on the left in Figure 17-6) beneath the words "How are you connected to the Internet?" your EDGE, 3G, or Wi-Fi speed is recorded for posterity. Then, if you tap the Results button that appears (and also appears on the front page of the site), you see the average speeds for all network tests — all Wi-Fi tests and EDGE tests in this figure, as well as all 3G tests which you can't see in the figure.

Figure 17-6: The network speed for this test was 735.4 kbps (left).
Average speed for all network tests: Wi-Fi, EDGE, and 3G (right).

What can we discern from all this? Well, our Wi-Fi speed of 735.4 kbps is slightly faster than the average Wi-Fi test speed over the past week. Put another way, our Wi-Fi connection is a little bit faster than the average Wi-Fi network.

Read Your Fortune

"Your great attention to detail is both a blessing and a curse." "It takes more than good memory to have good memories." "There is a true and sincere friendship between you and your friends."

Profound thoughts, huh?

We picked up these pearls of wisdom at iPhone Fortune Cookie 1.0 at `http://m.digitaljoven.com/fortune/index.html`. When you first arrive at this amusing site, you see the fortune cookie shown at the top of Figure 17-7.

Then when you rotate the phone to landscape mode, the cookie breaks in half and your fortune is revealed, as shown in the figure on the bottom. Repeat this little drill to request another fortune. Alas, some of the fortunes are as stale as the cookies we've eaten in real Chinese restaurants. Samples: "A pleasant surprise is in store for you." "You will live a long, happy life."

Guess that's just the way the cookie crumbles. (Hey, we couldn't help ourselves.)

Figure 17-7: Your fortune is hidden inside this cookie until you rotate your iPhone sideways to break it in half.

Ten Helpful Hints, Tips, and Shortcuts

*A*fter spending a lot of quality time with our iPhones, it's only natural that we've discovered more than a few helpful hints, tips, and shortcuts. In this chapter, we share some of our faves.

©iStockphoto.com/Skip ODonnell

Do the Slide for Accuracy and Punctuation

Here's a tip that can help you type faster in two ways. First, it helps you type more accurately; second, it lets you type punctuation and numerals faster than ever before.

Over the course of this book you've found out how to tap, how to double-tap, and even how to double-tap with two fingers. Now we want to introduce you to a new gesture we like to call the *slide*.

To do the slide, you start by performing the first half of a tap. That is, you touch your finger to the screen but don't lift it up. Now, without lifting your finger, slide it onto the key you want to type. You'll know you're on the right key because it pop ups — enlarges.

First, try the slide during normal typing. Stab at a key and if you miss, rather than lifting your finger, backspacing, and trying again, do the slide onto the proper key. Once you get the hang of it, you'll see that it saves a lot of time and improves your accuracy as well.

Now here's the best part: You can use the slide to save time with punctuation and numerals, too. The next time you need to type a punctuation mark or number, try this technique:

1. **Start a slide action with your finger on the *123* key (the key to the left of the Space key when the alphabetical keyboard is active).**

   This is a slide, not a tap, so don't lift your finger just yet.

2. **When the punctuation and numeric keyboard appears on-screen, slide your finger onto the punctuation mark or number you want to type.**

3. **Lift your finger.**

The cool thing is that the punctuation and numeric keyboard disappears and the alphabetical keyboard reappears — all without tapping the *123* key to display the punctuation and numeric keyboard and without tapping the *ABC* key (the key to the left of the Space key when the punctuation and numeric keyboard is active).

Practice the slide for typing letters, punctuation, and numerals, and we guarantee that in a few days you'll be typing faster and more accurately.

Auto-Correct Is Your Friend

Here are two related tips about auto-correction that can also help you type faster and more accurately.

Auto apostrophes are good for you

First, before moving on from the subject of punctuation, you should know that you can type *dont* to get to *don't,* and *cant* to get to *can't.* We've told you to put some faith in the iPhone's auto-correction software. And that applies to contractions. In other words, save time by letting the iPhone's intelligent keyboard insert the apostrophes on your behalf for these and other common words.

Assault on batteries

Because this is a chapter of tips and hints, we'd be remiss if we didn't include some ways that you can extend your battery life. First and foremost: If you use a carrying case, charging the iPhone while it's in that case may generate more heat than is healthy. Overheating is bad for both battery capacity and battery life. So take it out of the case before you charge it.

If you're not using power thirsty 3G or Wi-Fi networks, or a Bluetooth device (such as a headset or car kit), consider turning off the features you don't need in Settings. It could mean the difference between running out of juice and being able to make that important call later in the day.

Activate Auto-Brightness to enable the screen brightness to adjust based on current lighting conditions. Using this setting can be easier on your battery. Tap Settings on the Home screen, tap Brightness, and then tap the On/Off switch, if necessary, to turn it on.

Turning off Location Services (tap Settings, tap General, and then tap the On/Off switch to turn Location Services off) and Push (tap Settings, tap Fetch New Data, and then tap the On/Off switch to turn Push off) can also help to conserve battery life.

Finally, turning on EQ (see Chapter 7) when you listen to music can make it sound better, but it also uses more processing power. If you've added EQ to tracks in iTunes via the Track Info window, and you want to retain the EQ from iTunes, set the EQ on your iPhone to flat. Because you're not turning off EQ, your battery life will be slightly worse. But your songs will sound just the way you expect them to sound. Either way, to alter your EQ settings, tap Settings on the Home screen, tap iPod, and then tap EQ.

Apple says a properly maintained iPhone battery will retain up to 80% of its original capacity after 400 full charge and discharge cycles. You can replace the battery at any time if it no longer holds sufficient charge. Your one-year limited warranty includes the replacement of a defective battery. Coverage jumps to two years with the AppleCare Protection Plan. Apple will replace the battery if it drops below 50% of its original capacity.

If your iPhone is out of warranty, Apple will replace the battery for $79 plus $6.95 shipping, plus local tax, and will also dispose of your old battery in an environmentally friendly manner.

We're aware of at least one exception. The iPhone cannot distinguish between *it's,* the contraction of "it is," and *its,* the possessive adjective and possessive pronoun.

Make rejection work for you

Along those same lines, if the auto-correct suggestion isn't the word you want, instead of ignoring it, reject it instead. Finish typing the word and then tap the *x* to reject the suggestion before you type another word. Doing so makes your iPhone more likely to accept your word the next time you type it, and less likely to make the same incorrect suggestion again.

Here you thought you were buying a tech book, and you get grammar and typing lessons thrown in at no extra charge. Just think of us as full-service authors.

Three Ways to View the iPhone's Capacity

When your iPhone is selected in the source list in iTunes, you see a colorful chart at the bottom of the screen that tells you how your iPhone's capacity is being used by your media and other data.

By default, the chart shows the amount of space your audio, video, and photo files use on your iPhone in megabytes (MB) or gigabytes (GB). But you knew that. What you probably don't know is that when you click the colorful chart, it cycles through two more slightly different displays. The first click changes the display from the amount of space used to the number of items (audio, video, and photos) you have stored. Click once more, and the display changes to the total playing time for audio and video, as shown in Figure 18-1.

This is particularly helpful before you go on a trip. Knowing that you have 5.6 hours of video and 1.8 days of audio is far more useful than knowing how many gigabytes you're packing.

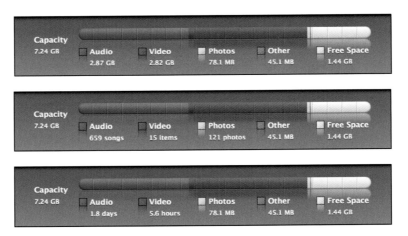

Figure 18-1: Click the colorful chart, and what's stored on your iPhone is expressed in different ways.

So You Want to Sync Notes, Do You?

As you've no doubt discovered by now, there's no easy way to synchronize notes between iPhone's Notes application and your computer. There are some third-party apps that synchronize notes between your computer and iPhone or a Web page — Evernote, OmniFocus, FileMagnet, and Jott, to name a few — but none of them synchronizes notes between computer and phone for free.

So, if you'd like to sync a note or notes, we know of a kludge that won't cost you a penny. Forget about using the Notes application or any notes application and use your contact manager program and the Contacts list in the Phone application. You see, each contact has its own notes field, and each notes field can contain a decent amount of text.

So the kludge is to create a fake contact or contacts and use their notes fields for notes you want to sync. Then, after you sync, and assuming you remember the names of your fake contacts — try AAA for the first and last names so the note appears as the first item in the alphabetical contact list on your iPhone — your notes will be on both your phone and your computer.

It may not be the most elegant solution, but it does work — and best of all, it's free!

Tricks with Links and Phone Numbers

The iPhone does something special when it encounters a phone number or URL in e-mail and SMS text messages. The iPhone interprets as a phone number any sequence of numbers that looks like a phone number: 1-123-555-4567, 555-4567, 1.123.555.4567 and so on. The same goes for sequences of characters that look like a Web address (URL), such as `http://www.WebSiteName.com` or `www.WebSiteName.com`. When the iPhone sees what it assumes to be a URL, it appears as a blue link on your screen.

If you tap a phone number or URL sequence like the ones just shown, the iPhone does the right thing. It launches the Phone application and dials the number for a phone number, and it launches Safari and takes you to the appropriate Web page for a URL. That's useful, but somewhat expected. What's more useful and not so expected, is the way Safari handles phone numbers and URLs.

Let's start with phone numbers. When you encounter a phone number on a Web page, give it a tap. A little dialog box appears on the screen displaying that phone number and offering you a choice of two buttons: Call or Cancel. Tap Call to switch to the Phone application and dial the number; tap Cancel to return to the Web page.

Here's another cool Safari trick, this time with links. If you press and hold on a link rather than tapping it, a little floating text bubble appears and shows you the underlying URL.

You also see the underlying URL if you press and hold on a URL in Mail or Text. We find that having this information provided here is even more useful because it enables you to spot bogus links without switching to Safari or actually visiting the URL.

Finally, here's one last Safari trick. If you press and hold on most graphic images, a Save Image button appears. Tap it and the picture is saved to the Camera Roll in the Photos application.

Share the Love

Ever stumble on a Web page you just have to share with a buddy? The iPhone makes it dead simple. From the site in question, tap the + button at the bottom of the browser. Then tap the Mail Link to this Page button that appears on-screen. When you do this, a mail message appears with the subject line pre-populated with the name of the Web site you're visiting, and the body of the message pre-populated with the URL. Just type something in the message body (or don't), supply your pal's e-mail address, and tap the Send button.

Choosing a Home Page for Safari

You may have noticed that there's no home page Web site on the iPhone version of Safari as there is in the Mac and PC versions of the browser (and for that matter every other Web browser we know of). Instead, when you tap the Safari icon, you return to the last site you visited.

The trick is to create an icon for the page you want to use as your home page, and the technique is called creating a *Web clip* of a Web page. Here's how to do it:

1. **Open the Web page you want to use as your home page and tap the + button.**

2. **Tap the Add to Home Screen button.**

   An icon that will open this page appears on your Home screen (or one of your Home screens if you have more than one).

3. **Tap this new Web clip icon instead of the Safari icon, and Safari opens to your home page instead of to the last page you visited.**

Figure 18-2: Notice that the My Home icon appears where Safari usually appears in the dock.

TIP

You can even rearrange the icons so that your home page icon, instead of the Safari icon, appears in the dock (the bottom row that appears on every home screen), as shown in Figure 18-2. See the tip in Chapter 1 for rearranging icons if you've forgotten how.

Storing Files

A tiny Massachusetts software company known as Ecamm Network is selling an inexpensive piece of Mac OS X software that lets you copy files from your computer to your iPhone and copy files from the iPhone to a computer. (There is no Windows version.) Better still, you can try the $19.95 program called PhoneView for a week before deciding whether you want to buy it. Go to www.ecamm.com to fetch the free demo.

In a nutshell, here's how it works. After downloading the software onto your Mac, double-click the program's icon to start it. To transfer files and folders to the iPhone (assuming there's room on the device), click the Copy To iPhone button on the toolbar and click to select the files you want to copy. The files are copied into the appropriate folder on the iPhone. Alternatively, you can drag files and folders from the Mac desktop or a folder into the PhoneView browser.

To go the other way and copy files from your iPhone to your computer, highlight the files or folders you want copied, and click the Copy From iPhone button on the toolbar. Select the destination on your Mac where you want to store the files and then click Save. You can also drag files and folders from the PhoneView file browser onto the Mac desktop or folder. Or you can double-click a file in the PhoneView browser to download it to your Mac's Documents folder.

If you need access to the files on your iPhone, or if you want to use your iPhone as a pseudo-hard disk, PhoneView is a bargain.

Create Ringtones for Free in GarageBand

Though it was beyond the purview of the ringtone discussions earlier in the book, it is relatively easy to create free iPhone ringtones with Apple's GarageBand application (which is bundled with every Mac). Start by launching GarageBand and creating a new Music project. Then:

1. **Click the Media Browser button to reveal the Media Browser pane.**

2. **Click the disclosure triangle to reveal the contents of your iTunes library.**

3. **Click your iTunes music library to reveal its contents.**

4. **Click the song you want to turn into a ringtone and drag it onto the timeline (*Hello Muddah, Hello Faddah!* in Figure 18-3).**

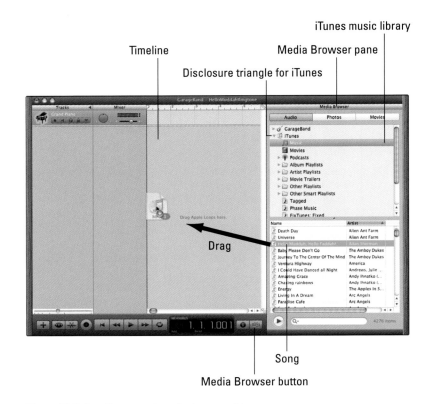

Timeline

Media Browser pane

iTunes music library

Disclosure triangle for iTunes

Drag

Song

Media Browser button

Figure 18-3: Creating a custom ringtone, part I.

You can't use songs purchased from the iTunes store for ringtones because they are protected by Apple's digital rights management copy protection. GarageBand won't let you drag a protected song onto its timeline. So you can make ringtones only out of songs you've ripped yourself from CD or downloaded without rights management or other copy protection (such as MP3s from Amazon.com).

5. **Click the Cycle Region button to enable the Cycle Region.**

6. **Click in the middle of the Cycle Region and drag it to the portion of the song you want to use as your ringtone.**

7. **Fine-tune the beginning and end points by clicking and dragging the Cycle Region's left and right edges, as shown in Figure 18-4.**

Cycle Region beginning

Cycle Region end

Cycle Region

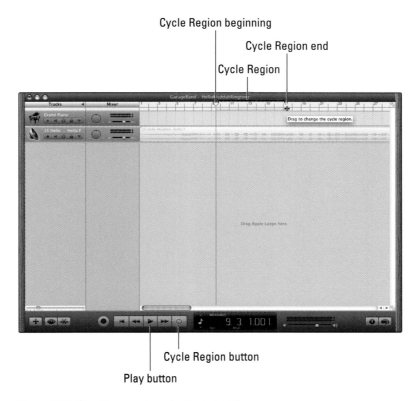

Cycle Region button

Play button

Figure 18-4: Creating a custom ringtone, part II.

For best results, keep your ringtones under 30 seconds.

8. Click the Play button to hear your work. When you're satisfied with it, choose Share⇨Send Ringtone to iTunes.

The next time you sync, your new ringtone becomes available on your iPhone. To use it as your ringtone, tap Settings, tap Sounds, tap Ringtone, and then tap the ringtone in the list of available sounds. To associate it with a specific contact or contacts, find the contact in either the Contacts application or the Phone app's Contacts tab, tap Ringtone, and then tap the ringtone in the list of available sounds.

Taking a Snapshot of the Screen

True confession: We threw in this final tip because, well, it helps people like *us*.

Permit us to explain. We hope you've admired the pictures of the iPhone screens that are sprinkled throughout this book. We also secretly hope that you're thinking what marvelous photographers we must be.

Well, the fact is, we couldn't take a blurry picture of the iPhone using its built-in (and undocumented) screen-grab feature if we wanted to.

Press the Sleep/Wake button at the same time you press the Home button, but just for an instant. The iPhone grabs a snapshot of whatever is on the screen.

The picture lands in the iPhone's Camera Roll, from where you can synchronize it with your PC or Mac, along with all your other pictures. And from there, the possibilities are endless. Why, your picture could wind up just about anywhere, including in a *For Dummies* book.

Index